USERS
NOT CUSTOMERS

USERS

NOT CUSTOMERS

Who Really Determines the Success of Your Business

AARON SHAPIRO

PORTFOLIO/PENGUIN

PORTFOLIO / PENGUIN
Published by the Penguin Group
Penguin Group (USA) Inc., 375 Hudson Street, New York, New York 10014, U.S.A.
Penguin Group (Canada), 90 Eglinton Avenue East, Suite 700, Toronto, Ontario,
Canada M4P 2Y3 (a division of Pearson Penguin Canada Inc.)
Penguin Books Ltd, 80 Strand, London WC2R 0RL, England
Penguin Ireland, 25 St. Stephen's Green, Dublin 2, Ireland
(a division of Penguin Books Ltd)
Penguin Books Australia Ltd, 250 Camberwell Road, Camberwell, Victoria 3124, Australia
(a division of Pearson Australia Group Pty Ltd)
Penguin Books India Pvt Ltd, 11 Community Centre, Panchsheel Park,
New Delhi—110 017, India
Penguin Group (NZ), 67 Apollo Drive, Rosedale, Auckland 0632,
New Zealand (a division of Pearson New Zealand Ltd)
Penguin Books (South Africa) (Pty) Ltd, 24 Sturdee Avenue,
Rosebank, Johannesburg 2196, South Africa

Penguin Books Ltd, Registered Offices: 80 Strand, London WC2R 0RL, England

First published in 2011 by Portfolio / Penguin, a member of Penguin Group (USA) Inc.

10   9   8   7   6   5   4   3   2   1

LIBRARY OF CONGRESS CATALOGING-IN-PUBLICATION DATA
Shapiro, Aaron.
    Users, not customers : who really determines the success of your business / Aaron Shapiro.
      p. cm.
    Includes bibliographical references and index.
    ISBN 978-1-59184-386-3
    1. Customer relations. 2. Consumer satisfaction. 3. Information technology—Management.
4. Internet marketing. 5. Electronic commerce. I. Title.
    HF5415.5.S5196 2011
    658.8'12—dc23   2011023391

Printed in the United States of America
Set in Adobe Garamond Pro   •   Designed by Spring Hoteling

For Carolyn

CONTENTS

Users First

If You're Not Thinking About Users, You'll Soon Be Out of Business

My wife loves seltzer water. I can't stand it, but she will hardly drink water if bubbles aren't in it. So I thought it'd be great to buy her a soda maker. One afternoon, I passed by a Williams-Sonoma store and decided to stop in. Lo and behold, they had one sitting on the shelf: a SodaStream Genesis drinks maker for $150. But it seemed expensive. I could buy her a pantry full of 150 bottles of premade seltzer for that price. So I decided to shop around.

I opened the RedLaser app on my iPhone and used it to scan the machine's bar code to find out what other retailers charged. Bed Bath & Beyond carried the same thing for a hundred dollars. Success! Fifty dollars in savings. I waved down a sales clerk and showed her my findings. But she declined to match the price.

So right there, in the middle of a beautiful Williams-Sonoma store in a high-rent location on the Upper East Side of Manhattan, I bought the SodaStream Genesis drinks maker—from Bed Bath & Beyond by using my mobile browser.

Companies such as Williams-Sonoma are in for a rude awakening. One day everyone will shop this way, and companies will either change their ways or be out of business.

Twenty years ago, purchases were driven by television ads, the selection of stores in the local town center or nearby mall, the brands those stores carried and the prices they charged. "Shopping around" meant traveling from store to store or calling down a list of retailers in the Yellow Pages. This is the antiquated environment in which most companies are still built to thrive.

In one short generation, we've seen a dramatic shift in how we buy things as well as how we interact with companies, do our jobs, and communicate with each other. Digital technology has quickly become so pervasive that it's rare for any personal or business interaction to begin anywhere else.

We are often introduced to new people through e-mail or an online community. After a phone call or in-person meeting, we maintain contact through digital channels, whether it's e-mail, instant messaging, or Facebook. In three years, texting is expected to surpass voice usage on cell phones. The same goes for how we learn about companies. If we're job hunting, we may find opportunities through a career site such as Monster or a jobs search engine such as Indeed. We maintain our résumés on LinkedIn, because that's where recruiters go to initiate interactions with us. If we're shopping, we may be introduced to the product by Googling, by noticing its newest promotion on a Groupon e-mail alert, or by seeing something listed on a product comparison site such as TheFind. Already 41 percent of all offline retail purchases in the U.S. begin with Internet research, and 7 percent of all retail commerce is now transacted online. In 2012, the total of these two figures is expected to reach 50 percent, which is equal to $1.2 trillion of digitally driven consumer spending. We're entering an economic environment in which the majority of our transactions begin with digital. In this context, there is no such thing as an offline business; everything is a digital business.

Beyond our social lives, careers, and consumer behavior, digital services also power our information gathering: we learn the news from our e-mail accounts, Twitter, Web sites, and apps; we find out the weather by installing a widget on our desktop or by opening "The Weather Channel" app on our phones. Digital technology helps us figure out where we are on the globe and where we need to go; it's how we count calories, read books, deposit checks, maintain grocery lists, and listen to the radio. In the always-on environment of the Internet and smart phones, we constantly rely on digital services and products to accomplish our everyday tasks. In a typical day, I use more than a hundred Web sites, apps, and digital services made by at least twenty-five different companies.

Businesses must keep up with these changes or else risk becoming the next Circuit City, Polaroid, or Blockbuster—companies that, thanks to digital technology, are either out of business or just a shadow of their former selves.

At HUGE, the interactive agency I run, we spend a lot of time thinking about these issues, and how companies should respond to this new business reality. When our clients first approach us they're asking for many different things—a new Web site, a mobile app, a social media campaign—but they're actually asking for the same thing: digital transformation. They need to renew their company to fully compete in this new economy, and are asking for our help in making the shift. Through my work at HUGE, my colleagues and I have had the privilege of studying the inner workings of many blue-chip companies across a diverse array of industries. We work with their leadership to help formulate the correct strategy, organizational structure, and business processes to compete in the digitally driven marketplace. When looking back at our years of inside access, what's most striking is that the issues facing companies and the effective solutions are remarkably similar regardless of industry or organizational size. To validate and challenge the patterns we observe in the field, we embarked on a quantitative study to help answer the question: what drives success in today's digital-centric business environment?

Our first step was to identify a large pool of companies and pick out the ones that used digital technology effectively, proactively, and progressively: what I call the "Digital Leadership Set." We began our search for these companies with the Fortune 1,000—the thousand largest companies in America. Recognizing that it might not be all that fair or accurate to compare the digital progressiveness of, say, a petrochemical company with a pure technology play such as eBay, we broke up the group into nineteen industry sectors. Then, for each sector, we evaluated the twenty largest companies.

More than sixty aspects of each company's digital footprint were systematically examined. We measured the degree to which digital is effectively used across all aspects of their businesses: sales, marketing, customer service, human resources, and the core products and services the companies offer. This information was then aggregated into an overall digital excellence ranking (1–100). The top performers were named members of the Digital Leadership Set—the group of companies that consistently performed better in the digital environment than their peers.

For 2011, these companies are:

Amazon	Hewlett-Packard	Southwest Airlines
American Express	The Home Depot	Staples
Apple	IBM	Target
Best Buy	JetBlue Airways	Walmart
Dell	Macy's	Washington Post Company
FedEx	Microsoft	Wells Fargo
Google	Sears Holdings	

Next, we researched the organizational structures, management styles, and strategies shared by the leaders. We wanted to identify the qualities that determined stellar digital performance and differentiated the winners from the losers. Not only did we want to understand their approach to digital from an organizational and management standpoint; we wanted to see how digital integrated with different aspects of their business, from sales and customer service to product development and marketing.

The Digital Leadership Set survey added a much-needed level of nuance and rigor to what I already suspected from my consulting work: the companies that were most successful in this new economic order consistently prioritized the needs and interests of the people who interacted with them through digital channels—their users. True market leaders focus on meeting user needs above all else. Keep users happy, and customers follow; grow your user base and your customer base grows as well.

USERS MATTER

Users are the customers, employees, job candidates, business prospects and partners, brand fans, members of the media, and other influencers who interact with a company through digital media and technology. This may be through an intranet, a mobile app, an online job application form, a Web site, customer relationship management software, a Facebook page or Twitter account, or any other element of a company's internal and external digital footprint. In short, users are defined as anyone who interacts with a company through digital media and technology.

fig. 2

PARTNERS   INFLUENCERS

PROSPECTS   **USERS**   EMPLOYERS

BRAND FANS   JOB CANDIDATES

CUSTOMERS

2. Users vs. Customers

There are lots of different types of users, and while they each have their own distinct interests and objectives, they all want digital tools to easily and quickly give them a leg up. These tools might include a database management program that makes it easier to identify actionable insights, or a mobile app that helps you keep better track of when you last fed your newborn.

It's the same for users who are also customers. They use digital media and technology to empower them to make the right purchases, and smarter purchases than if they were limited to the local mall. They research products online by reading user reviews and professional reviews, and by asking the advice of their social network; they compare prices across a universe of sellers no matter their geography and then don't blink at purchasing an item with the click of a button, even if that button is on a phone. These digital customers are a whole different animal than what existed when adages such as "the customer is king" and "the customer is always right" were taught in Business 101. Today, a customer must be thought of in a new way: as one segment of users, one of the many types of people who interact with your company through the digital version of your organization. And they all want digital technologies to make their lives easier and better.

The key to success is focusing on this broader user base. Customers will naturally follow. Thanks to social media, bloggers and "friends" all combine to create a large swarm of public opinion that shapes brands and drives sales. Your employees, business partners, and pool of new job prospects are also influential users who help operational performance, and they shape brands and drive sales as well. Users can also be more intimate with and influential on a company than anyone who has completed a purchase. And if you need numbers to convince you, in terms of volume, a company's user base often vastly outweighs its customer base. Focus just on pleasing the person who opens his wallet and you're missing out on the real windfall.

USERS WANT EASY

How do you attract users, engage with them, and develop long-term relationships with them? Give users the one thing they all want: simplicity. That's it. People use technology to do things, to accomplish tasks—whether to look up some sports scores, e-mail a friend, watch a video, or research which new shoes to buy. When a user interacts with a company through digital technologies, she wants it to be simple and effortless, because she just wants to accomplish what she set out to do. She doesn't want to spend even a second wondering how a Web site works or what to click on next; she just wants it to happen. If it doesn't, she'll reject you.

I've seen it time and again through HUGE's vast amount of research on user behavior. When people find something difficult or confusing to use, they don't blame the company that made the digital product, they blame themselves. They get frustrated and think they're too stupid to figure out how to use it. People don't like feeling stupid, so they usually reject the entire experience. They'll say how much they hate the app or Web site, shut it down, and refuse to look at it again.

Because it is difficult for a company to get a second chance, the stakes are very high. Companies must spend a lot of time thinking about *usability*—how easy it is for people to use a digital product, and how satisfied users are with their experiences. The best user experiences require no directions or learning curve; the technology just works the way in which people expect. So for all companies, usability—and an organization's consistent ability to achieve a high level of usability excellence—is a critical driver to success.

THE USER-FIRST COMPANY

The importance of users is so profound that a new model has emerged for business excellence: what I call the user-first company. Today's most successful companies organize their business around users and building user satisfaction. Users are then the engine for growing a customer base and the overall organization. This new user-first way of doing business affects every part of the organization: how companies approach sales and marketing, their organizational structure—really, every aspect of their operation.

Through the Digital Leadership Set survey and HUGE's work with clients, I've pinpointed an overall management framework that governs the way in which user-first companies operate.

The operations of any company can be split in two: internal drivers,

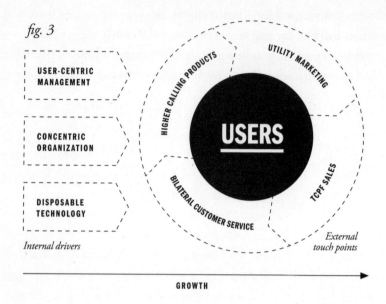

fig. 3

USER-CENTRIC MANAGEMENT

CONCENTRIC ORGANIZATION

DISPOSABLE TECHNOLOGY

HIGHER CALLING PRODUCTS

UTILITY MARKETING

USERS

TCPF SALES

BILATERAL CUSTOMER SERVICE

Internal drivers

External touch points

GROWTH

3. The User-First Company

which govern the overall operations of the company; and external touch points, which is how the company connects with the outside world. For user-first companies, the user is at the center of all external touch points; the focus of all attention. Internal drivers are oriented toward pushing the external touch points forward, propelling growth. Let's take a quick look at each area to see how the framework operates.

Internal Drivers:

- **User-Centric Management:** This is a philosophy and approach to management that puts users first in all decision making. These managers use research and market insights to develop frictionless digital interactions between the company and its stakeholders. They anticipate user needs and meet them. This ethos is coupled with the talent to bring these effective digital initiatives to life. Part of this is being a "visionary pragmatist"—someone who is able to build a vision of digital excellence that galvanizes the broader organization, and yet who still has the pragmatism to get the job done. Anyone can spout out a bunch of grand ideas; a user-first manager knows to evangelize only what he or she can actually accomplish.

- **Concentric Organization:** Organizations are typically faced with a chronic shortage of digital talent and a workforce comprised of varying comfort levels with technology. To bridge these talent hurdles, the best companies embrace a "concentric" organizational approach. A small centralized team develops an infrastructure that allows large numbers of nontechnical employees to use digital tools to advance their business goals. The infrastructure also standardizes the external user's experience. This is how many of the most successful products of digital-only companies such as Facebook, Twitter, and YouTube are developed and maintained. A talented few control a standard experience that is easily used by millions of individuals to communicate.

- **Disposable Technology:** With the Internet evolving so quickly, companies must build internal- and external-facing digital solutions that are easily disposed of, evolved, and replaced. By maintaining a "disposable" and therefore nimble approach to technology, organizations avoid large investments and initiatives that prevent them from making rapid changes.

Effective user-centric management, concentric organization, and an agile approach to technology position a company to more successfully execute the external touch points of the user-first strategy. External touch points consist of the four places people outside of the organization interact with any company: marketing, sales, customer services, and the actual product and service sold. We find unique patterns to how these external touch points operate in a user-first landscape:

- **Higher Calling Products:** A user's true needs are generally greater than what a particular product can solve. Items such as toothpaste, diapers, espresso, and credit cards incrementally improve quality of life, but user-first companies aspire to solve their users' higher-order problems. They don't just do this through aspirational brand promises. User-first companies often integrate digital services into their products to create a combined digital and analog offering that's more valuable to customers than the physical product alone. I call this a company realizing its "higher calling." It becomes the way companies resonate more powerfully with their users and customers, and combat the incredible breadth of competition and tremendous pull of commoditization in the online marketplace.

- **Utility Marketing:** Users don't want to be interrupted by irrelevant, unhelpful marketing messages. So user-first companies market themselves in a way that's helpful to their audiences. Brand awareness and sales are achieved not through traditional advertising, but by developing brand-relevant programs that help users accomplish the task at hand.

- **TCPF Sales:** Users decide when and where to buy by evaluating four factors: trust, convenience, price, and fun (TCPF). Each person places different levels of importance on the four different areas, and a user-first company responds to this challenge by optimizing TCPF for its business and its target users' particular needs.

- **Bilateral Customer Service:** When it comes to customer service, many users want the most comprehensive, automated, self-service solution possible. But when the need strikes, they also want extremely high levels of human customer service. This seemingly bipolar attitude means user-first organizations must take a bilateral approach to keeping customers happy. It may sound like a tall order, but it's worth it. Good customer service becomes great marketing as people spread positive words about your business. Do a bad job and it can quickly spiral into a public relations nightmare.

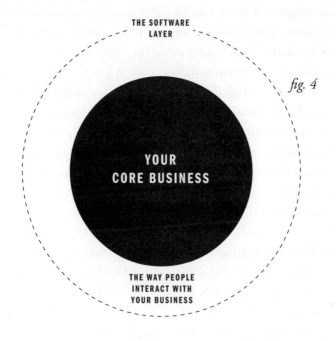

^{4.} *The Software Layer*

THE SOFTWARE LAYER

When the seven principles are executed in sync, a user-first company can almost be seen as a business sheathed in a layer of software through which nearly all user interactions occur.

This software "layer" requires consistent and intensive oversight, because user expectations will only increase. As businesses offer new and improved, more user-friendly solutions, users realize that they can expect more, placing increasing demands on your company and others. I call people who today are in their early twenties "post-digitals" because they never knew life without the conveniences brought by digital technology. By the time they become primary breadwinners and decision makers, a company that has ill-managed its software layer is at risk of becoming obsolete. When this generation becomes adults maintaining households and running companies—whether they're shopping for a book or making a multimillion-dollar-enterprise purchasing decision—they will embrace the products and services of a firm with a top-of-the-line, friendly, easy-to-use software layer. And they will be quick to dismiss a firm with a software layer that's out of date and inefficient.

Put more bluntly, the quality of a company's digital presence will only become increasingly important. It will surpass the significance of a company's physical sales force, presence at a university job fair, calendar-wielding secretaries, human receptionists, and traditional marketing and advertising. In some of these cases, digital technologies have already usurped brick-and-mortar tactics. The software layer is quickly becoming the beating heart of the company.

Managers of user-first companies therefore have two businesses to look after: the core business they've always overseen and the software layer that connects the core operation to its users. Ignore the software layer and you ignore your users; ignore your users and you risk losing your business.

In action, software layers are the amalgamation of various technologies all programmed to work in concert to streamline and automate operations. For example, HUGE has a top-notch internal software layer. Because of it, all I need to get my work done is a MacBook Air and iPhone. I don't have filing cabinets, an assistant, or a landline phone. My calendar is maintained digitally and shared with the company. In fact, everyone in the office can access each other's calendars, eliminating the time-consuming back-and-forth of scheduling meetings. The majority of communications between employees happen via instant message and e-mail. The conference rooms are regularly used for group phone calls, but almost no one uses his or her desk phones. Documents and other files are shared via Google Docs and similar services. Time sheets are filled out online, as are tech support and meeting room requests. There's literally a tier of digital technologies running the whole agency, and it allows us to run ourselves nimbly, to collaborate, to save time, and to work effectively. External interaction is no different: client interaction, recruiting, and new client communications all happen digitally. And HUGE isn't an ultramodern anomaly. The software layer is the norm; the challenge for companies is how to create it, maintain it, and evolve it at the pace of user expectations.

USER-FÍRST MEETS CORPORATE AMERICA

The concepts behind a user-first company and the software layer are starting to penetrate mainstream business, in industries and organizations where you'd least expect it.

On its face, Procter & Gamble is no Google. The 174-year-old company sells toothpaste, soap, deodorant, batteries, cleaning products, paper towels, and other traditional, utilitarian home products. Many of its brands—including Crest, Ivory, Tide, and Charmin—are so old that your great-grandmother bought them when she went shopping. It's the largest advertiser in the world, and its advertising strategies have long represented, if not defined, the norm: thirty seconds of network television airtime used to tell memorable stories. Its primary customer is not you; it's Walmart. But P&G and its brands are clearly on their way to becoming wholly user-first.

The company's move to a more user-first focus started with the commitment to prioritize customers. Over the last decade, P&G recovered from a period of revenue decline by creating products that met or exceeded customer needs. A. G. Lafley, the top leader at P&G throughout most of the 2000s, led with the motto "The Consumer Is Boss." Accordingly, P&G's investment in market research is unmatched. The company interacts with more than five million people in nearly a hundred countries and spends more than $400 million per year, all to increase consumer understanding. But when Lafley left the helm, P&G was again struggling to keep up with competitors. Current chairman and CEO Bob McDonald looked to improve the company's fortunes by aggressively pursuing an increased presence in digital media. In his 2010 letter to shareholders he pledged to make P&G "the most digitally enabled company in the world." He wanted to heavily digitize the company and connect with consumers on a one-to-one basis. In other words, he was setting a directive for the company to prioritize users.

The company's top digital executive from 2008 to May 2011, Lucas Watson, clearly championed a user-first mandate. At a 2009 conference of the Interactive Advertising Bureau, he told the crowd, "You need an ideal and an idea. An ideal is a sense of calling, a sense of purpose, a higher reason for being than just trying to sell the next case of diapers."

This is a direct call to identify and meet real user needs, rather than act self-servingly and push a hard sell. One example of this user-first mentality in action is Charmin's partnership with SitOrSquat. The P&G brand sponsored an iPhone app where users can log in and review publicly accessible toilets, and where users who need a clean bathroom, say with baby changing facilities, can go to find out where the nearest adequate facility may be. With digital technology, Charmin is literally helping users go to the bathroom.

Perhaps the best-known instance of P&G's user-first foray into digital media was the 2010 effort to advertise Old Spice body wash. What started out as a traditional Super Bowl commercial featuring the Old Spice man, "the man your man could smell like," morphed into an outstanding social marketing campaign that inserted itself into the consciousness of users around the globe. It was so funny, users welcomed it into their lives, rather than treating it as an ad to be avoided. The campaign culminated with the production of hundreds of short videos responding to user questions that were produced in real time over just a few days. This effort generated more than two billion media impressions.

E-commerce is another way P&G is making striking moves toward prioritizing user interests above all else. Let's say you're on the Gillette Web site and you decide you really want a Fusion ProGlide Power Razor. You don't have to log off and hope your local Walgreens has it in stock. There's a buy-now button on the site that when clicked presents a list of all the e-retailers selling the item. This feature is available on many P&G brand sites. What's more, one e-retailer on the list is one you might not expect: P&G itself. In May 2010, P&G launched its own e-store. In doing so, P&G is taking another step toward prioritizing the needs of users—many of whom want the convenience of buying direct—at the expense of retailers, who today represent P&G's primary customer base.

That being said, P&G isn't yet a full-fledged user-first company. It still has a way to go, particularly in its reliance on institutional, proprietary technology solutions rather than on nimble, disposable ones. But it's definitely on its way. Industries undergo different stages of digital transformation at different times. Products such as books that are extremely standardized were the first industries to be transformed by e-commerce, for example. Consumer packaged goods (CPGs), on the other hand, are standardized, but also very convenient for most people to purchase locally, and usually people want to use the product immediately—not an option when buying online. This is one reason CPGs haven't been the earliest adopters of e-commerce. Other industries, by virtue of product and service complexity—or the power of entrenched interests—have focused their user-first activities not on direct sales but on brand building. Change, however, is coming to everyone.

BEGINNING THE JOURNEY

One of the most surprising things new employees find when they start at HUGE is that many big companies don't know what to do online. From the outside, we all imagine that famous, billion-dollar businesses function like well-oiled machines and completely understand digital media. But when one looks inside, many of these firms are struggling to adjust to the new economy—in spite of the successful management and incredible revenue stream that got them to household-name status in the first place. These firms may all be great at what they do, but since digital isn't a core competency, they can struggle with it.

If you feel as if your business is not effectively leveraging digital, you are not alone. A user-first strategy may seem like a faraway, idealistic goal, but you can probably say the same thing about your competitors or any other peer companies. Moving toward a user-first strategy is a big way for organizations to propel growth.

User-first is a management philosophy, not solely the province of engineers who build software. You don't need to know a lot about technology to understand and learn from the chapters that follow. By putting the right management approach in place—which really boils down to accepting that the people who interact with your company online are the most important thing—your entire company can transform and succeed in our digitally driven economy.

If you're an entrepreneur, this book can help you too. In today's environment, a user-first approach is key to the success of literally any start-up. We talk about only a few start-up companies in this book—Diapers.com and Mint.com, for example—but candidly, I could have made every example a different start-up company. More often than not, start-ups are doing things the right way.

Entrepreneurs are the great agents of change in our society. They make user-first management a necessity to every business, because if the existing, big-name companies don't do it themselves, entrepreneurs will come along and sweep them out of business. Some companies are motivated to change because of opportunity. But most change because of this fear.

Whether you're part of a large company or the head of your own shop, the user-first company framework can help you create a high-performing organization that's in tune with how people want to do business. Indeed, think about your own interaction with the user-first companies such as Best Buy, Zappos, or Digital Leadership Set organizations. They're probably the companies you prefer to do business with yourself.

In the following chapters, we'll explore how this user-first approach manifests across all aspects of a business, exploring in depth the seven internal and external principles of the user-first company framework. I hope that when you finish reading this book, you'll have the knowledge you need to effect positive, user-first change in your organization.

1

User-Centric Management

How to Build a User-First Mindset in Your Company

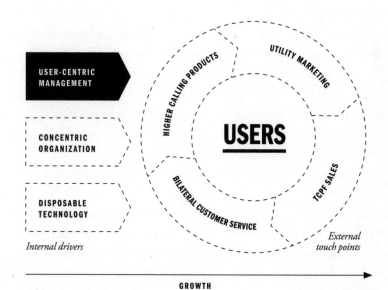

Aaron Patzer was a cog in the Silicon Valley technology machine. An engineer by training, he had stints at IBM and a research firm specializing in network communications. And like many coders, he had the start-up bug.

Patzer, however, was different from the average techie dreamer. He had started nurturing his entrepreneurial ambitions as a teen in the 1990s, and he was a stickler about his personal finances. When most kids were baby-sitting and mowing lawns for spending cash, he was developing Web sites for local businesses in his hometown, Evansville, Illinois. He tracked the ebb and flow of his money with Microsoft's Money program and Intuit's personal finance software, Quicken. Throughout college and grad school, he continued to keep a close eye on his spending, updating his Quicken books every week.

But then after a couple of years in the workforce, for the first time in years, he fell behind on his bookkeeping. This break in routine served as his wake-up call.

On the Sunday in late 2005 that he decided to catch up, he synced Quicken with his accounts and downloaded about five hundred transactions. Quicken could only autocategorize 40 percent of them, leaving several hundred transactions he would have to address individually. Then he tried Microsoft Money, which could only autocategorize about 15 percent of them. This was going to take him a whole afternoon, and all he wanted to know was how much he was spending on gas and groceries. Then it hit him: Quicken is not quick. It's slow, difficult to use, and saddled with too many unnecessary features that get in the way.

In spite of this weakness, Quicken had long dominated its industry. It could boast a 70 percent share of the personal finance software market starting in the early nineties and extending into the new millennium. In 2007, it still boasted fifteen million users who had spent thirty dollars to a hundred dollars on the product. But the bulk of financial software users—high net-worth men between the ages of forty and sixty—didn't know any better. Quicken and its competitors were still simpler than balancing a checkbook and categorizing expenses by hand.

But Patzer, born in 1980, had likely never had to manage his finances by hand. Neither did many other young adults. In fact, much of the up-and-coming class of consumers had grown up with online banking, debit cards, and ATMs—for them Quicken would have been the laborious old-school way of working. Patzer imagined an entire swath of American consumers would welcome a streamlined personal finance program, a tool that would allow them to check in on their finances from anywhere they had an Internet connection. In Patzer's view, managing your money shouldn't be a chore. It should be a service. It should be "so easy to use, people will actually use it," he said.

So he quit his job and got to work on what would become Mint.

In about a year and a half after leaving his job, Patzer was ready to present his product. His biggest breakthrough was developing an algorithm that accurately and reliably matched up 85 percent of all transactions with their appropriate spending categories, drastically reducing the painstaking task of entering data. Immediately Quicken and its ilk were antiquated.

For much of the other necessary technology, Patzer relied on existing tools. To access all of a user's expenses, which often included transactions across several accounts at various financial services companies, he teamed up with Yodlee, a business-to-business company that already offered this type of account aggregation service to banks. For other software needs, he used publicly available open-source solutions whenever possible. This allowed Patzer to focus on the big-picture issues, such as Mint's business model.

As part of his aim to make personal finance effortless, he decided to make the service available online and free of charge. So, as many other online businesses do, he turned to advertising as a source of revenue. But rather than simply deciding to sell space for flashy banner ads, he pushed the idea further. Mint's advertising messages would be tailored to each user, and each message would provide information that could save that user money. For example, if a Mint user had money in a savings account at a low-interest rate, Patzer's service would suggest another bank with a much higher interest rate and show a calculation for how much more the user could earn in interest. Or, say the system recognized that the user traveled a lot. The program might then recommend a credit card with a more generous frequent-flyer miles program. For each user that clicked through and opened an account with a sponsor, Patzer stood to make a twenty-dollar to sixty-dollar referral fee. He had devised a win-win situation: the service would literally, genuinely serve users and could still generate ample revenue.

The other major challenge was getting the first users. Because revenue from this innovative advertising plan would only be available with an existing audience, Patzer had to drum up a strategy for his own initial promotion on a shoestring budget. Rather than paying for traditional online advertising, Patzer started a blog on the Mint site. Every week, the blog posted a feature called "Train Wreck Tuesdays" that shared people's personal finance disasters. Another recurring post asked tech celebrities and personal finance bloggers what was in their wallet. Rather than blatantly selling to users, this material engaged them and gave them a few minutes' worth of entertainment, or in the case of Train Wreck Tuesdays, the comforting feeling that you're not alone if you're struggling with your finances. It also served to add more visibility in search engine results because there was now more Mint content for Google and its competitors to link to. But Patzer's blog strategy didn't end there. He also attracted guest posts from existing personal finance bloggers. These guest bloggers logically would bring their readers with them, readers who were already interested in personal finance and Internet savvy—Mint's target audience. About nine months out, he started soliciting e-mail addresses for early Mint access. When the sign-up list exceeded the capacity the site was equipped to handle at launch, he asked bloggers if they'd put an "I Want Mint" badge on their blog in return for priority access. This built consumer awareness as a form of free advertising and still more visibility in search engines.

Patzer officially launched Mint in September 2007 at the TechCrunch 40—an annual demonstration of start-ups put on by the TechCrunch blog—and he won the award for best presenting company. It came with $50,000 and ample free publicity. Mint began an astounding trajectory. Within six months, it had more than 200,000 users and was adding 10,000 new ones every week. The typical click-through rate (the number of users who click on an ad divided by the number of times users had opportunities to see the ad) was an astoundingly high 12 percent on Mint—the more typical click-through rate for banner ads is 0.2 to 0.3 percent. This provided Patzer with a strong strategy for revenue generation and his users an average of $1,000 each in savings.

Intuit soon became his direct competition. In early 2008, the parent of Quicken branched out beyond boxed software and launched Quicken online. For use of this tool, Intuit charged consumers thirty-six dollars per year. This fee, Intuit argued, allowed the site to survive without advertising revenue and therefore guaranteed the service was free from any conflicts of interests. This strategy proved unpopular. So Intuit switched to a free model. But none of this reined in Mint's momentum. After two years in business, Mint had attracted 1.7 million users, with seven hundred thousand of them active in any given month. They were young— the average age was around thirty—and about 40 percent were female. These were two demographics personal finance software products had formerly ignored. Patzer had essentially uncovered a whole new market and in turn began to steal future customers from Quicken and Microsoft Money.

The older players weakened from the competition. Microsoft Money quickly gave up. It announced in June 2009 that it would be discontinued. Quicken Online did put up a fight. It could boast 1.5 million users, but still it had only a hundred thousand active users on a monthly basis. Eventually Intuit did what any multibillion-dollar business does when it sees an extraordinarily successful newcomer on its territory. It bought Mint in September 2009 for $170 million. Patzer took a position with Intuit as vice president and general manager of the company's personal finance group, overseeing the company's Mint and Quicken products for desktop, online, and mobile. One of his first actions was to announce the end of Quicken Online; its customers would be transferred to Mint.

In less than three years, Patzer had gone from being just another Silicon Valley engineer to single-handedly battling a software giant with annual revenues of more than $3 billion—and winning his fight.

THE TRIUMPH OF USABILITY

Mint's win over Quicken reflects a profound change in technology over the last decade—the triumph of usability. The companies that have become the most successful online provide users with digital experiences they like and even love. It's not just about a Web site being mindlessly easy to navigate or a product being intuitive to use (although that's part of it); it's about providing convenience, satisfaction, pleasure, or a serendipitous, valuable discovery for the user.

This is exactly what Patzer prioritized. He started with the goal of designing a program that he would want to use, and its success was driven by millions of individual users wanting to use it too. His achievement stemmed directly from his commitment to an easy, pleasurable user experience. Much of the technology powering his system had already existed. His multimillion-dollar step forward was combining those technologies into a user-friendly package.

The significance of this retooling is apparent in the fortunes of Yodlee—the company whose behind-the-scenes technology helped make Mint happen. Twelve years after its founding and $116 million in fundraising later, the firm has yet to have an exit event. Infrastructure is not where the real value is captured in the digital space. Instead, it's the company that focuses on the enjoyment of its users first and foremost. Companies such as Oracle, Cisco, EMC, and Akamai—which specialize in building complex, often hard-to-use technological infrastructures for businesses—have greatly benefited from the digital revolution. But even Oracle, the strongest performer in the group with a stock price increase of about 140 percent over the last five years, can't match the growth and value creation of the companies that really prioritize the user. Amazon, one of the Digital Leadership Set companies, has seen its stock price more than quadruple over the same period of time.

Patzer is not the only one who recognized this marketplace reality. YouTube had a similar strategy, said TechCrunch founder Michael Arrington. YouTube didn't invent online video or even user-generated video. Adobe's flash technology did most of that heavy lifting. But YouTube put a pretty face on it, made it easy for everyone—from children to grandmothers—to use, and then sold out to Google for $1.65 billion. And there's more. Twitter, TiVo, Nintendo Wii, Apple, and virtually every other big technology success in the last decade have been driven by usability. These companies made information gathering, communication, social life management, video recording and sharing, TV watching, video game playing, and movie watching much easier and more enjoyable than the existing solutions. This also extends to business services: think Salesforce.com for customer relationship management; Amazon Web Services for technology infrastructure; Google AdWords for advertising. In fact, in my observations of successful Internet companies, it's clear that almost without exception, usability and strong user-centric experiences have been a key factor in their success.

Usability is so powerful that a strong Web presence can shine even if the original offline business is in shambles and the economy is in a severe recession. That's what happened to Gap Inc.

In the 1990s, Gap was undeniably cool. Movie stars, supermodels, and almost everyone else in the country donned Gap brand clothing. But in November 2001, Gap Inc.—which includes the Banana Republic and Old Navy brands—posted its first quarterly loss in more than a decade. Gap brand store sales in North America dropped 12 percent and Old Navy North America stores' sales dropped 13 percent. Fingers pointed at the company's aggressive expansion and its poor choices of newer styles. The company as a whole is still plagued by lukewarm sales. Between 2004 and 2010, the best year for Gap Inc.'s comparable store sales was the single year it managed to grow by 1 percent.

In 2003, however, the e-commerce side of the business began an impressive turnaround. That year Gap Inc. hired Internet entrepreneur Toby Lenk to run its online operations. He championed usability. He studied the in-store experience, watching how quickly and smoothly women shopped and decided to re-create this seamless experience online. He told *The New York Times* in 2005, "When a woman walks into one of our stores, she can process things really quickly. Like when she's browsing the racks, she takes a quick look at what the sizes and colors are, picks up something and keeps going." On the existing site, this activity would have required dozens of clicks on pull-down menus for size, color, and style. Then once the item was selected, the online shopper would have been whisked away to the checkout page. Imagine this in the retail location. It would be ridiculous if each time a shopper put an item into a cart, he or she were pushed up to the cash register. (This is still what happens on many e-commerce sites, by the way.) So to better match the online experience with the brick-and-mortar, physical one, he redesigned the site to let shoppers see larger pictures of products by rolling over them with their mouse, no clicking necessary—more akin to quickly perusing a rack at the store. And then he used a pop-up window to show shoppers they had placed an item in their shopping bag, rather than moving them out of their shopping experience.

Three years later Lenk took another great stride. In 2008, Gap Inc. pulled together its brands, including its flagship Gap, Banana Republic, Old Navy, and online shoe-store PiperLime onto a single Web site. In 2009, it added Athleta, which sells women's athletic clothing. For the first time, customers could shop for all Gap Inc. brands at a one-stop shop with one shopping cart and one shipping fee—without driving to a shopping mall, hunting for a parking spot, studying the directory, and hoofing it from one store to the other with bags in hand—the inconvenient portion of the brick-and-mortar experience. The result? The company's Web traffic grew almost immediately by 8 percent and the number of items sold per transaction increased by 10 percent. In 2008, the same year we fell into the great recession, U.S. apparel sales online grew only 6 percent, according to market research firm comScore. Gap Inc.'s e-commerce division? It grew 14 percent and surpassed $1 billion in online sales. Lenk prioritized usability and kept his business in the black when everyone else's (including Gap Inc.'s own physical stores) were struggling.

The triumph of usability. It sounds straightforward: make something people enjoy using and they'll use it more. It's been a selling point for products and services since the beginning of time. Think about Ivory soap. Its big sales pitch in the early 1800s: it floats! It doesn't need to be searched out from soapy, dirty water. It's convenient. It's more enjoyable to use. Consider cashmere. People love to wear cashmere because it feels soft to the touch and adds significant warmth without bulk. In this case enjoyment comes from quality. Enjoyment can also come from avoided disasters. Hefty sells its garbage bags by bragging about how easy they are to close, how strong the plastic is, and how they get rid of odors. Enjoyment can even stem from the cachet of the brand name itself: Gucci handbags are valued higher than a plastic shopping bag not only because they're made well but because of the pride and happiness a woman feels while wearing the Gucci logo. Soft drinks are perhaps the best example of all. In their advertising campaigns, they rarely talk about being tasty, carbonated sugar water. They sell refreshment, altruism, and happiness.

FORM OVER FUNCTION

But for the technology sector, usability did not triumph until recently. For a long time, function has reigned over form, and user experiences have been mediocre at best. In the 1980s, people couldn't program their VCRs. Today they can't find all the TV shows they might want to watch using the slow, confusing "guide" menus provided by cable television providers. It's also apparent in hundred-page user manuals for devices and the everlasting challenge of doing a large mail merge in Microsoft Word. Technology has long been about what the product could do, not how enjoyable or easy it was for people to use. This is no longer true, and Microsoft's evolution over the last few years underscores this shift.

Microsoft's primary customer for its software has been other businesses. Its first-ever major break was licensing its MS-DOS operating system to computer manufacturer IBM for inclusion in its first personal computer. In 2010, its three largest operating segments, which include divisions that sell Windows and Microsoft Office and account for approximately 80 percent of its revenue, largely serviced business needs.

When a company sells technology products to businesses, its customers are information technology (IT) departments, not individual lay users. This means the products are tailored to the concerns of the company, and the result is software that has been designed with function over form. A purchasing department's top concern is that the software or hardware has the features everyone in the business needs to do his or her job. Software manufacturers are therefore incentivized to produce and offer products brimming with features. The more features a product contains, the more likely the product is to match the requirements outlined by a company's CIO.

Microsoft Office is a prime example of this. Think about all the pull-down menus, all of the decisions required to make a chart in Excel and all of the complex keyboard shortcuts, all of the tools you've probably never used in Word, and all of the "wizards" intended to help simplify complex features. Anything a business user might ever need to do in a word processing, spreadsheet, and presentation program is inside Office's walls. But just as with Intuit's Quicken, too many features makes software excessively confusing for the average user. Next consider Windows. At its foundation, Windows is the graphic face of the computer's text-based internal functions. Its core purpose is to make computers useful for those who aren't particularly tech savvy. But for the life of the product line, users have only been able to get the user experience they want (such as limited alerts, display preferences, and faster boot-up time) if they could successfully navigate several layers of operating system files and then skillfully adjust settings labeled with tech jargon. Most users aren't computer science majors and aren't able to do this, but this didn't prevent Microsoft from thriving. After all, Microsoft sold to the IT departments, and IT department staffers were computer geeks at heart. Microsoft just needed to sell the product by demonstrating functionality and reliability, which it did fabulously.

Apple, in contrast, has focused on selling its own hardware and software to individual consumers. As a result, usability has always been its chief concern, as consumers had to love the product enough to buy it themselves and spread the word. When you look at its products, the focus on user enjoyment—a marrying of form and function—is obvious. Apple was the original player to market a graphic operating system with the Mac; then it went on to revolutionize personal electronics with the iPod, iPhone, and iPad.

In spite of Apple's focus on usability, throughout the 1980s and 1990s it stayed many steps behind Microsoft in terms of financial performance. But as digital became a consumer lifestyle, Apple started winning. In late 2010, for the first time in the companies' histories, Apple passed Microsoft in market capitalization—$222 billion to $219 billion.

Apple's triumph isn't just a testament to the explosion of mobile and the consumerization of digital; it's had profound effects on how technology is used and purchased within an organization. Over time, consumer interest in Apple products translated into the same people demanding usable products in the business environment; just as a generation ago personal instant messaging led the way for corporate adoption of the technology. In mid-2010, Apple announced that more than 80 percent of Fortune 100 companies used the iPhone and about 50 percent of the Fortune 100 were testing out or already using the iPad.

And so while Microsoft remains a massively successful and profitable seller of enterprise software—let's not forget that Microsoft Office and Windows alone generate significantly more revenue than all of Google—Microsoft's hegemony has been chipped away by the call for usability, and usability is starting to become a driver for technology decisions within the enterprise as well. Microsoft was forced to change, and its newfound user-first approach has resulted in the Windows 7 Phone and desktop OS, and recent innovations such as the Xbox Kinect. What's even more interesting is that Microsoft products aren't just mimicking Apple; they're actually pushing the envelope of design, trying new things in an unending quest to meet user needs.

When form triumphs over function even at places like Microsoft, it's time to think closely about the technology in your organization and how users—internal employees as well as external constituents—are able to successfully and unsuccessfully interact with it. As user tolerance for "figuring it out" continues to decline, companies have no choice but to focus on the experience.

USABILITY IS EVERYWHERE

The importance of usability goes beyond customer-facing businesses; indeed, it's had a big impact on almost every kind of business, even organizations that only serve other companies.

PCH International, a $125 million supply chain management company with operations largely based in China, produces computers and electronics for some of America's biggest PC and electronics brands. You very likely own a gadget made under contract by PCH. While its business is making physical objects and sending them around the world, its lifeblood pumps through digital technologies. Journalist James Fallows visited the plant for an article in *The Atlantic*. There he watched as an order from Palatine, Illinois, was fulfilled with near immediacy. Seconds after the midwestern user clicked the buy button, "the order appeared on the screen 7,800 miles away in Shenzhen. It automatically generated a packing and address slip and several bar-code labels." With this level of automation and simplicity, the factory workers were able to get the order out on the next Federal Express pickup. It would arrive on an Illinois doorstep in forty-eight hours. This supply chain stretches across the world and yet it requires no real human-to-human interaction, nor any real technical expertise from its main users (the buyer and the fulfillment workers). It's just that easy to use.

The company's competitive intelligence and sales are also based in digital technologies. Fallows described a "Google Earth–like system" that can illustrate the Chinese marketplace of manufacturers. "You name a product you want to make—say, a new case or headset for a mobile phone. [The company founder] clicks on the map and shows the companies that can produce the necessary components—and exactly how far they are from each other in travel time." The user can then click on a site to see photos, read information about the management, or maybe even watch a video of the working assembly line. Other programs let the company track its products around the world on ships, planes, or trucks, and monitor the volume of items in its warehouses. PCH's software has streamlined processes and facilitated information gathering that formerly required extensive coordination by employees, if it was available at all. Because of the software layer, PCH's system is seamless, fast, accountable—and very desirable.

Google has a product called Adwords that's another example of usability in a business-to-business environment. Adwords is the program through which advertisers buy sponsored ads that show up in its search results—it earned Google $23 billion in 2009. To place an ad in Google searches, advertisers don't need to call a Google salesperson. They just have to go online and follow some tutorials and prompts. Small advertisers can have their ads live within minutes. Larger advertisers looking for more personalized service can ask an engineer to tweak the Adwords interface so that it's more effective and efficient for their needs. Google does have a sales staff, but they do not have to be active in each individual transaction. Consider how this differs from newspaper ad sales, where each paper has an army of salesmen boasting circulation figures and acting as the high-priced liaison between advertiser and publisher. At Google, the easy-to-use advertising product sells and implements itself.

For these two very different companies, usability is key. They are so easy to use and so seamless, their reach so extensive, it's simply easier and more effective to do businesses with them. Usability from digital technologies often translates directly to lower costs and higher sales. Today's business environment demands a frictionless interaction between company and customers. Interaction through software—no humans required—is business at its most efficient. The most usable companies with the best software are the ones that win.

THE EVOLUTION OF MANAGEMENT

This triumph of usability—and broader organization of a company toward meeting user needs—begins with management. Management must have the expertise, wherewithal, and philosophical approach to run a business that is centered around the user. To understand how user-centric management differs from the other forms of management, it's helpful to picture it as an evolution of management styles that's become increasingly market driven over time.

Of this pyramid, the least market-responsive management style is continuity-centric. These types of companies are generally run by bu-

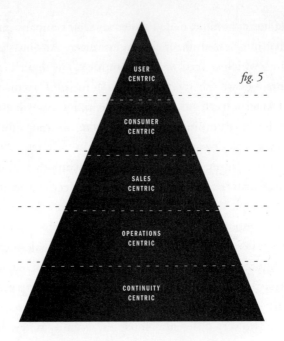

^{5.} *Hierarchy of Management Styles*

reaucracies that have a strong, entrenched market position in their field. Management typically focuses on continuing the status quo. For example, think of Exxon Mobil, the largest publicly traded company in the world. A descendant of John D. Rockefeller's Standard Oil empire, Exxon Mobil remains extremely profitable by focusing on oil and gas exploration, refining, and sales around the world. Company management has beat back several recent shareholder initiatives that would have compelled the company to begin to factor climate change and renewable energy into its company strategy. CEO Rex Tillerson has stressed Exxon is solely in the oil and gas business; any deviation would be counterproductive. When you have a strong lead in the market and can regularly report windfalls of revenue, good management is management focused on avoiding change.

The operations-centric style of management is all about staying competitive by finding efficiencies. It's found in highly competitive sectors, where to retain profitability and market share, the company must streamline its supply chain and operations in every way possible. Examples of operations-centric businesses include the three giant health-care supply-chain companies in the United States: Cardinal Health, McKesson Corp., and AmerisourceBergen. Among them, they control 90 percent of the market keeping hospitals, pharmacies, and doctors' offices stocked and ready every day to meet patient needs.

Companies that focus on driving sales, boosting short-term revenue, and closing the next deal follow the sales-centric style of management. I always think of SAP and Oracle, the two aging lions of enterprise software that offer database management, sales tracking, and CRM systems, as prime examples. They employ large teams of commissioned salespeople who focus on selling the newest iterations of the software to corporate IT management. They're great at selling. They have to be; these firms develop feature-laden products that are often a nightmare to use.

I doubt there is a CEO alive who doesn't refer to his or her company as "customer driven." It's often a meaningless claim. But some management teams are genuinely customer-centric. They focus on listening to customers, meeting their needs, and developing their products and messaging accordingly. The prime example is Procter & Gamble. Under the leadership of A. G. Lafley, as discussed in the introductory chapter, P&G lived by the motto "The Customer Is Boss," and created products that met or exceeded customer needs. To accomplish this, it more than quadrupled its design staff, partnered with outside design firms for product development, and started an initiative to send teams home with customers to see how they actually use P&G products. One result: after a team watched someone use a screwdriver to pry open a box of Tide, they made the product easier to open.

User-centric management is the natural evolution of a customer-centric management style, but optimized for the digital age. It acknowledges the incredible influence of the company's digital footprint and ensures all management decisions are focused on keeping users first. User-centric managers make sure every digital touch point of their company is user friendly, intuitive, and frictionless. The net result for companies that make this happen is more sales, lower costs, and improved efficiency. This is the management style I see consistently in companies that are most successful in the digital arena.

MANAGING WITH THE USER IN MIND

So how do user-centric managers actually operate? How do they view their jobs? What obstacles do they face? Peter Scherr has served in digital leadership roles at Digital Leadership Set members American Express and JetBlue Airways, as well as Warner Music Group, among other major companies. His experience can answer all of these questions.

Scherr joined JetBlue in 2004 as director of interactive marketing. At the time, the five-year-old airline was getting a lot of good press because it was an airline customers enjoyed using. It was celebrated for having friendly service, relatively roomy leather seats, and personal TVs for every flyer. Scherr was mainly responsible for the company's Web site, which was also highly regarded and heavily trafficked—80 percent of JetBlue tickets were booked through the site. But when Scherr looked at it from a usability perspective, he saw ways it could be improved. For example, the home page didn't feature fare specials, something that customers were always interested in. Answers to common questions were difficult to find. The surprisingly popular, "How do I travel with my pet?" likely cost JetBlue millions in the time spent on customer-service phone calls dedicated to that inquiry. "It was the type of thing where this beautiful site, this simple site, was not quite as simple and beautiful as you might imagine," Scherr says.

To pinpoint areas of improvement, Scherr launched an intensive research project. The company held focus groups where participants were given a pile of index cards, each labeled with an activity, such as booking a flight or checking a flight's status, and asked to physically map out how they'd like to navigate the Web site. A research team then went to Jet-Blue's Salt Lake City customer-service center and listened in on customer calls, logging what people liked about the airline, what they didn't like, and their common questions. Another team studied the Web site analytics data. (Site analytics present managers with quantified details about user behavior including the various ways users get to the site, the geographic regions where users are located, and which pages they tend to leave the site from.) In this case, the JetBlue team mapped where people click to determine which areas of the site people used the most and how they navigated them. Scherr then presented all of this qualitative and quantitative data to the senior management and asked for the budget to do a redesign. They signed off.

The new JetBlue.com launched in October 2006. It featured bargain fares in a large font on the home page, an easy-to-use flight booking tool that catered to new users but also let advanced users jump right in, and a new online baggage-check option that became extremely popular. To further define the brand as user-centric, the home page featured beautifully shot photos of the company's customers using its JFK terminal. But one of the biggest contributions to JetBlue's efficiency was its improved FAQ (frequently asked questions) page. JetBlue made sure that all of the most common questions people asked when calling customer service were clearly answered online, which included installing a small box on the right side of the FAQ page listing the five most-asked questions. After the launch, inquiries to customer service plummeted. Paying attention to what users really wanted had paid off.

In 2007, Scherr left JetBlue to become vice president for interactive marketing at Warner Music Group. Unlike JetBlue, which was riding high, Warner, along with the rest of the music industry, was straining to remain profitable and relevant as CD sales waned and illegal downloads picked up. One way Warner hoped to adapt was by signing artists to "360" deals. These would allow labels to take their traditional cut of CD and digital sales, but would also entitle them to a share of ticket sales, merchandise sales, endorsement deals, and other sources of revenue that rely on the use of an artist's brand or music. In exchange, record companies would take a more active role in managing the careers of their artists, including helping them build their Web sites and digital strategies. Scherr was responsible for direct-to-consumer digital strategy—and he had one shot to shine.

At the time, most artist Web sites were pretty simple. Most were derived from the art and layout of the latest album cover and press photos. Scherr approached the "360" initiative by asking, "What would the fans of an artist like to see on a Web site?" To answer the question, he did something unheard of in the record industry. He held focus groups with fans. And they taught him a winning insight: they desperately wanted a direct and authentic connection to their favorite musicians.

So he gave it to them. First he picked a band—the alternative rock group Paramore. Then he partnered with a firm selling technology that made it easy for people to post and share photos and videos taken with their mobile phones. Band members took to it immediately. They started to upload photos of themselves goofing around backstage, practicing their instruments in rehearsal studios, and generally being themselves. "That became the magic of the site, being fun and engaging for fans," Scherr says. "All of a sudden it didn't look like manicured, premeditated, professional photos and videos—it was real content from the source, and fans couldn't get enough. They were commenting about it, they were freaking out about it, sending it around the Internet." Because each photo was watermarked with the Paramore.net Web address, even illicit copies ended up sending fans back to the official Web site. The Paramore site became so popular it set the standard against which all of Warner's other artist Web sites were judged.

Scherr's success with Warner stemmed from the same strategy that he had used with JetBlue. It was all about putting users first.

THE KEY ATTRIBUTES OF A USER-CENTRIC MANAGER

Successful user-centric managers adhere to four key rules:

1. **Have the discipline to say no.** Saying no goes against the natural tendencies of a leader who would like to encourage creativity and inspire the team to think of all the great elements a product could have. But generally, the best products are those that focus on one true user need and have simple features that meet that one essential need. Fewer features mean you can focus on making each one really great—and then you also have less to build and users have less to learn. It's faster for you and them.

During the JetBlue redesign, people asked Scherr to add more and more features. But he knew saying yes to them all would result in a cluttered Web site with decreased usability. "It's hard when people want to get involved with their piece of the pie and want to get it addressed and you have to say no," he says. "In the end, it serves everybody well to do that, but it was hard."

2. **Make process king.** User-friendly managers must, as part of their job, launch digital initiatives. By definition, these projects are logistically intensive. They require research, technology development and partnerships, visual design, user-experience design, copywriting, quality assurance testing, and more. The most successful user-centric managers are therefore very process oriented—if initiatives are not carefully planned and controlled, they can easily spiral out of control. If this happens, the manager fails because nothing can get done.

   It was vital that the relaunch of Paramore's Web site be timed to the release of their upcoming album. But that meant Scherr had to jettison anything that wasn't achievable on schedule. If the technology wasn't available to bring an idea to life, that idea had to be dropped. "If things were a little too ambitious, we said, 'Forget it, let's just keep moving,'" Scherr says. This approach kept the launch on time and within scope.

3. **Know enough to be dangerous.** The best user-centric managers must be able to critically evaluate the recommendations of experts and technicians in every stage of development from technology and analytics to design and marketing— and make key decisions across all areas of their company's digital footprint.

   At Warner, Scherr needed to decide whether to build artist Web sites with open-source technology or to develop proprietary systems. The challenge was that Scherr's main area of expertise was marketing, not engineering. So he taught himself what he needed to know. This knowledge, he says, was vital. "You have to be conversant in technical issues and challenge people, because if you're not conversant at all, you could be smoke screened to death by highly technical people," he says. "The key is to always ask, 'So what?'" Scherr says. "As in, 'What does this buy us?'" And then be able to tell if the answer being given is sound.

4. **Couple pragmatic vision with evangelism.** Organizations look to user-centric mangers as leaders who articulate a compelling vision about where the Internet can take them. At the same time, the best managers are responsible enough to only propose ideas that can be realized. This balance results in smiles from the management for their inspirational ideas and the resources to work with to make them happen. The need is for evangelism joined with the necessary pragmatism to build consensus among stakeholders.

   When Scherr arrived at JetBlue, he found that no one had been looking at the data that documented user behavior on JetBlue.com. For example, hardly anyone knew such significant trends as what tickets customers were selecting and then failing to buy. So Scherr went to the revenue management team to talk about using this information for more strategic marketing and pricing. They, however, were resistant, given the unfamiliar nature of the data. So he put together a report and brought it directly to JetBlue's founder and CEO, David Neeleman. Neeleman listened and then led the rally call himself. "He ran around the building imploring people to learn the data and make it part of our core analysis," Scherr says. "I made people uncomfortable but I couldn't sit on this data and not evangelize it. It was just too significant. Within a couple of months, it ended up being a core part of our analysis."

THE USER-CENTRIC MANAGEMENT TRIANGLE

User-centric management is a careful balance of three sides of a triangle: user goals, business goals, and technical feasibility:

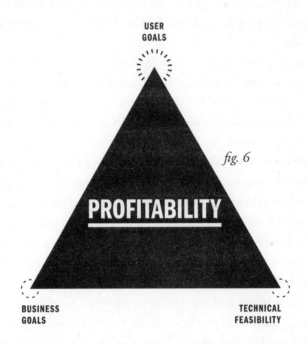

fig. 6

6. The User-Centric Management Triangle

- **User goals** are what users want—the tasks they want to accomplish by interacting with the organization and the need the digital experience should satisfy.

- **Business goals** are the specific corporate objectives with respect to users—for example, sell subscriptions or increase the average order price.

- **Technical feasibility** is critical because the proposed initiative must be brought to life. An idea is not enough; it must be able to be executed within budget and with available resources.

Generally speaking, these constraints are usually in conflict with each other. For example, users want everything to be free, but the business needs to be profitable. If the business is too focused on short-term revenue and it spits out constant, spammy sales pitches, it annoys users and loses their business. If the business decides to meet every user and business goal at the expense of what's technically possible, it gets nothing accomplished.

The art of great user-centric management is clearly defining user goals, business goals, and technical implications, and then carefully striking a balance between the three levers. When they're all in perfect harmony, profitability—the area "inside" the user-centric management triangle—is maximized.

User and business goals are often closely interrelated but the process to identify them and activate them can be quite different. Defining user goals begins with the company's identifying the most cursory definitions of who uses their digital experiences and why. If it is a jewelry store that also sells wholesale jewelry-making supplies, Web site visitors are likely consumers shopping for brand-name jewelry or professional jewelers looking to purchase spare parts. If it's a newspaper Web site it must cater to existing subscribers and business news readers who have not yet subscribed. Once these basic delineations are made, the company often engages in a series of "listening labs." Listening labs are typically one-hour, one-on-one sessions with a trained moderator and a member of the target audience. The subject is asked to conduct tasks online related to the digital product in question, and while he is doing so, he is talking through the problems and issues he is facing and how he goes about solving a particular issue. This allows the company to learn, for example, what information jewelry shoppers want to know or how smooth the process is for buying a newspaper subscription. This allows the user-centric manager to understand how she and her competitors meet user needs, and, perhaps more important, what user needs are unmet.

Often this process results in the creation of detailed personas. A persona is a model of a user that represents a group of actual users. Designers use them to better understand a user group's typical needs, goals and behaviors, and to make sure all of a user group's needs are met with the design solution. For example, a designer might think, "Is this something Sally would use?" If the answer is "not often," then the feature could be put on the back burner. If the answer is "yes, on every visit," then the designer knows to prioritize that function. This goes on for each feature according to the needs of each user group and the company's own interests. At the end, there is a clear list of must-have solutions, could-have solutions, and features on the chopping block. This is also the framework for having the discipline to say no. That gimmicky new feature upper management asked for? If it doesn't fit a key persona's interests, it's out.

Next, the user-centric manager must work with her team to define the business goals. This requires more thought and precision than simply saying we want to sell more diamonds and subscriptions. It calls for clearly defining what the company is concretely trying to accomplish with its digital footprint. Would success solely be measured in sales? If so, would it be measured in sales volume, frequency, revenue, or the percent increase from pre-redesign sales figures? Would it be measured in number of visitors? If so, unique visitors, repeat visitors, visitors from certain geographic locations, visitors buying products with a higher profit margin than visitors buying less profitable items? Identifying these key performance indicators would guide the success of the digital foray, and further allow the user-centric manager to evaluate what user needs should be met. For example, if it's found that the jewelry company wants to increase the revenue from wholesale purchases, the user-centric manager knows to prioritize the user needs of professional jewelers. If the newspaper wants to increase number of visitors of the demographic its advertisers deem most valuable, the user-centric manager knows to focus on the interests of those people in particular.

The final component is technical feasibility. What would it technologically take to bring to life the perfect user experience that would complement business goals? How hard would it be to meet unmet user needs? After a detailed assessment with engineers, a clear plan is put in place to define what can and cannot be realistically attained given time and money constraints.

Once this process is completed and the new experience is created, the user-centric manager's relationship to the triangle is not over. Digital initiatives that continually meet user needs and business goals must be consistently evaluated so opportunities for improvement can be identified and implemented.

TWO SCHOOLS OF USER-CENTRIC DESIGN

The practice of refining and sustaining the performance of a digital footprint by evaluating user behavior and making small deliberate changes is how Google designs its products.

Google's management puts every revision of its home page and every new product through a rigorous series of user tests. "We test everything at Google," the company says on its site. "While any company would prefer real-life data to hunches and guesses, Google is more focused than most (or any) on getting conclusive proof that a new feature or function improves the user experience. We release many of our products in beta on Google Labs to get this kind of feedback early in the process so that we can influence the design and iterate quickly. The ability to test lots of products and features on hundreds of millions of users is enormously valuable. This test-bed of users (otherwise known as google.com) provides Google with an incredible advantage over enterprise-only search vendors. Bad ideas can be discarded quickly and great ideas can be implemented rapidly, because we have confidence and data to show that they'll improve the user experience."

The goal is the most seamless product possible. Larry Page, the cofounder, says, "The perfect search engine would understand exactly what you mean and give back exactly what you want." But the way they get there is through a series of small, steady, iterative improvements on all of their products. Many of Google's improvements are so small they're not noticeable. One day Google's search results included video results instead of just Web pages. Another day the legendary algorithm was tweaked to produce slightly better search results for a certain subset of queries. Users don't often realize it, but the change is constant, gradual, and never ending.

There's no better way than the Google school of user testing and analytics analysis to iteratively improve a product or digital interface. You try many things, test all of them, see what quantitatively performs better, and then roll that feature out. Then you might do it all over again to see if you can move the needle one more time. Best of all, with this model design geniuses are not needed—just lots of testing and good number crunching. But the Google strategy has its flaw, and that flaw is an inability to make a big tectonic leap that can really change the game.

The big bang, rather, is Digital Leadership Set member Apple's business, a company driven more by inspiration than by analytics. While little about their development process is public knowledge, it's safe to assume most everything flows from the vision of Steve Jobs, a known fanatical perfectionist, and his outstandingly talented design team. "Our job is to take responsibility for the complete user experience," Jobs has said. "And if it's not up to par, it's our fault, plain and simple." This isn't to say that Apple eschews all user testing. It does do user testing, but the big ideas and the commitment to those big ideas are supported by the gut instincts of a core team. They have an idea, a vision of where technology and interface design should go, and they work to bring that vision to life—and when it does come to fruition it shifts global business as well as the daily lives of millions of users.

The inspiration-versus-analytics approaches to design can be seen as reaching a local maximum versus a global maximum. With a reliance on analytics, you can only refine something to reach peak usability and performance within a current design framework. This is the local maximum. But a constant stream of small updates will never get you the global maximum—a big new idea that ends up satisfying users in a revolutionary, never-before-seen way. To achieve a true breakthrough that lets you reach a global peak, you need to throw away all the rules, all of the preconceived, limiting notions of user behavior, and look at the big picture.

The trouble with this "global-maximum" strategy is that there's incredible risk. After one win audience expectation becomes incredibly high; success is based on out-of-this-world talent (the likes of which few companies can attract), and it's not very conducive to incremental product improvement. It's all about the big, risky, game-changing bangs. That's why Apple products get criticized for their inability to stand the test of time.

When the iPhone 3G and 3GS became cluttered with apps, the iPhone 4 and its operating system came out and offered folders—an arguably cursory and inadequate solution for app management. iPhoto has a similarly beautiful, intuitive interface, but it gets weighed down once users put multiple years' worth of photos in the program. Over time, Apple products become more complicated and clunky than their original, elegant simple design intention. In the best possible world, big inspirational ideas live side by side with small, analytics-driven refinement.

USERS FIRST IN THE C-SUITE

For many organizations user-centricity exists within the walls of the Web department—a silo closer to the IT team, which keeps busy adding printers and fighting viruses, than to the senior executives actually running the company. But in the more advanced, digitally savvy corporations, user-centric managers are starting to get the keys to corner offices and the opportunity to influence the broader organization. This organizational approach puts the users-first philosophy in a position to permeate the whole company's culture and way of thinking. It's an early trend, but it's starting to happen:

- Digital Leadership Set member Walmart promoted the CEO of Walmart.com, Raul Vazquez, to be the president of Walmart West, which includes twelve hundred stores in twenty-three states. The motive for the move? Bolster the performance of e-commerce by more tightly integrating it with the chain's retail operations. Today Vazquez has risen even higher on the ladder and is EVP, global e-commerce, and has developed markets including the U.S., Canada, and the U.K.

- Nutrisystem made Joe Redling, former chairman and CEO of AOL International, its CEO and chairman, a nod to the weight-loss company's increasing emphasis on interacting with customers through the Internet. Shortly thereafter, in 2009, it promoted digital executive Chris Terrill to be the company's chief marketing officer. In his two-year tenure in the position, Terrill oversaw a redesign of the company's e-commerce site (he has since left to become CEO of ServiceMagic.com).

- In June 2011, American Express, seeking to maintain its success in an era where technology is rapidly changing how people spend money, made a bold move. It hired Josh Silverman to become president of its U.S. Consumer Services business, which includes the American Express consumer credit card. Silverman was previously CEO of Skype, a senior executive at eBay, and a senior executive at one of the most successful technology venture capital funds.

- The Weather Channel appointed former AOL Media Networks president Michael Kelly to be its CEO—again to maximize the business across all its platforms: TV, Web, and mobile.

- Barnes & Noble took steps in this direction by promoting William Lynch, Jr., the executive responsible for Barnes & Noble's digital activities and the Nook, to become the overall company CEO. Exiting CEO Steve Riggio told analysts and the press, "In just a year, he has put our e-commerce business back on its fast-growth track and has helped us quickly establish the company as a major player in the rapidly growing e-book and digital content arena, securing important partnerships with major technology companies." Lynch's new job would now include the brick-and-mortar retail division. The goal: to strengthen the chain's "multichannel relationship" with customers.

To be most effective, a user-centric manager must have access to all parts of the organization. He or she must be able to ask the sales team for information about tactics and results, talk to human resources about recruiting challenges, discuss software purchasing decisions with IT, and even have the ear of administrative services if something like digitizing conference room scheduling is required—and all of these departments must be receptive to the ideas and opportunities for improvement the user-centric manager identifies. User-first managers realize user needs must be met throughout the company in addition to those of potential customers, job applicants, and other users beyond its walls. They also know the first concrete step to their goal is implementing concentric organization, to be discussed next.

CHAPTER SUMMARY: USER-CENTRIC MANAGEMENT

Market Insights

- Usability—the degree to which a company's products and services are easy to use and understand—has emerged as the most important driver in digital business success over the last decade. Usability will only become increasingly important to businesses as consumers continue to embrace digital technology throughout their lives, raising expectations for what constitutes an acceptable digital product in the home and work environments.

- Usability is becoming just as important as "feature checklists" in IT buying decisions. This, coupled with a new generation of engineers who appreciate the value of good design, is heralding a revolution in in-office computing.

- With digital fueling performance, the most usable companies win.

Strategic Imperatives

- A new management style—user-centric management—is embraced by the most forward-thinking companies to effectively manage in this new environment. User-centric management puts users at the center of all business decisions. This ensures the company's digital footprint is always optimized for frictionless transactions with users, whether in a marketing, sales, or customer-service context. One can think of user-centric management as customer-centric management for the digital age.

- Effective user-centric leaders possess several key attributes: the discipline to say no, an essential element in prioritizing what's really important for users and what's just a distraction; an extremely process-oriented mentality, realizing that the effective implementation of a digital product is a long, logistical march; a range of knowledge across a broad spectrum of technology and interactive marketing, allowing them to quickly vet and retain the right resources; and a unique ability to evangelize a vision for digital excellence throughout the organization that's pragmatic enough to actually be executable.

- Most effective user-centric leadership is an exercise in balancing user goals, business goals, and technical feasibility. Ignore one of them and the initiative fails because it either is rejected by the audience, doesn't advance the organization's business objectives, or can't be properly implemented from a technical standpoint given time and resource constraints. If the three are perfectly balanced, profitability is maximized.

- There are two proven approaches for designing a digital experience that meets user needs. One is analytics driven, where the product is incrementally improved over time based on quantitative data and testing. The other is inspiration driven, where "the big idea" emerges with a flash of insight perfectly solving a user problem that consumers couldn't even articulate in a focus group (think the invention of the iPhone). While analytics is more predictable and proven, the potential upside is limited. The best Digital Leadership Set companies strive to embrace both.

- Companies are starting to implement this new management style throughout the entire organization by moving user-first leadership from the interactive department to the C-suite. While this is still an early trend, look for it among true innovators.

2

Concentric Organization

The Secret to Structuring a Business
That Efficiently and Effectively Meets User Needs

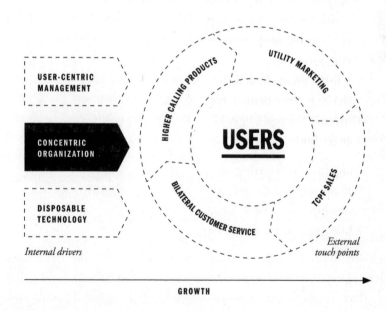

Leadership grounded in prioritizing users is a good first step, but it can only go as far as the organization's ability to execute. For many companies, execution in the digital arena is a challenge for one simple reason: a lack of talent and infrastructure.

The world's labor pool has not yet caught up to the Internet age, and the result is that despite an economic environment with generally high unemployment, companies have a chronic shortage of personnel suited to build high-quality digital experiences. In fact, four out of five businesses have had difficulty finding potential new hires who have both business and technical skills, according to a 2010 Forrester Research survey. And, nearly two-thirds of responding businesses found it difficult to find people with adequate customer and usability experience. This talent problem has only grown worse as communication mediums have continued to explode in diversity, requiring more specialized skills. Things were bad enough when companies only had to worry about Web sites. Now companies need social media specialists to handle Facebook and people who can devise an appropriate mobile strategy thanks to the proliferation of smart phones. The next missing skill set is only as far away as the next technology innovation. Lynne Seid, a partner in the global consumer marketing practice at the global recruiting firm Heidrick & Struggles, aptly called the situation, in regard to publishing companies, a digital talent emergency.

This talent dearth can't be allowed to prevent a company from communicating with its external audience via digital channels. Presence in the online, interactive environment is simply vital to survival. To endure in these conditions, companies must find a way to interact with their outside users in spite of the low digital literacy rate of their employee base. The answer can be found in the evolution of systems that empower laypeople to express themselves online.

Back in the early days of the Internet, communicating to the world through digital media was all about creating a Web site. But at first, this was incredibly hard to do. To create a personal Web site, the user needed technical expertise and server space. Novices couldn't do it, but they wanted to. To fill this need, services sprung up that offered people both a guiding structure and access to the essential resources for Web site development. Suddenly anyone could make his or her own site. GeoCities—founded in 1994 and purchased five years later by Yahoo for about $3.5 billion in stock—was one of the most popular programs of this kind. It offered any Internet user basic design tools and easily customizable templates, as well as server space, hosting, and a URL—literally everything anyone needed to put up his or her own Web site. Users had control over the entire design: you could select a background graphic like an outer space scene and then fill it up with things such as lightning bolts or yellow bricks; you could add lots of text in splashy colors such as red or green; and you could add flashing smiley faces, beating cartoon hearts, and blinking text to round out the page. By the time GeoCities was shut down in 2009, thirty-eight million Web sites had been created through this service alone.

The result, however, was far from an Internet populated with beautiful, user-friendly, fun-to-visit Web pages. Rather it became littered with millions upon millions of amateurish and unattractive sites. Then because none of them were as easy to update as a Twitter feed or a Facebook status update, no one kept them current. Each became a monument to a rare burst of enthusiasm. What's more, users had little impetus to visit each other's sites. GeoCities kept its thirty-eight million sites in a nearly unusable organizational structure. Search was not mainstream yet, and social networking as a tool for content discovery hadn't been invented yet. So who wanted to hunt down a poorly designed and outdated Web site? Nobody.

Then in January 2004 came MySpace. Similar to what was offered in GeoCities, MySpace let users choose their own color schemes and background graphics, alter the page structure, and add pictures and music players, flashing clip-art graphics, and links. But MySpace was different too: users could "friend" people, write on each other's walls, and easily post information. This gave MySpace the advantage of having regularly updated content, a way for people to find each other's musings, and a reason for people to visit each other's sites, even if the flashing bright red or blue-on-black text was hard to read. In the fall of 2005, nearly two-year-old MySpace could boast twenty-two million members. And GeoCities was on the precipice of a steep decline.

Then came Facebook. In 2005, Facebook was quickly expanding from its Harvard roots to the rest of the Ivy League, and to colleges around the country. It took a vastly different approach from MySpace. Mark Zuckerberg, Facebook's founder, stressed that Facebook should be seen as a utility. Its purpose, he said, was to link people with their friends. Creativity was curtailed. Facebook's site design was uniform and standardized across all users. Users had to work within a tightly defined structure—for the profile you filled out a form; to share something new, you wrote text and attached links, photos, and videos into one standard window. But that was okay with users because Facebook provided such a satisfying experience. For the first time, anyone could create an easily updatable online persona and keep up with old friends. The experience was so practical, no one missed having customizable backgrounds, layouts, and colors.

With Facebook's controlled gentlemanly experience on the market, MySpace, once the king of personal expression online, looked like an angry teenager in comparison. According to *Wired*, MySpace "encouraged creativity to the point of chaos." On MySpace, activities such as sharing news, photos, and links with friends were subservient to changing your page design and navigating through all your friends' crazy layouts. On MySpace, freedom of creativity trumped usability.

As we all know, MySpace lost the fight. In the summer of 2011, Facebook reached 750 million members while MySpace was sold for the fire-sale price of $35 million.

CONCENTRIC ORGANIZATION

The challenge corporations face today because of the talent drought and the critical need to create digital content mirrors the challenge that faced Mark Zuckerberg. He needed to devise a way to allow millions of lay users to communicate with each other and express themselves online while still maintaining a high-quality, usable environment. In his case, this was about connecting friends and empowering personal expression. In a corporation, employees need to interact with external constituents, such as potential new hires, new customers, and new business partners. In both cases, the quality of the experience is paramount. For Zuckerberg, it's what made Facebook so sticky and attractive to hundreds of millions of people. For every company, that experience becomes a part of its public brand, available to anyone with an Internet connection.

Zuckerberg—and the products that followed his strategy such as Twitter, Instagram, and Tumblr—made it easy for anyone, no matter how technologically illiterate, to effectively communicate online. They all offer users a tightly controlled environment for expression and interaction that is easy for consumers to use and enforces usability standards. This shell structure is what allows communications to thrive. Tools enabling unfettered creativity, such as those provided by Geocities and MySpace, don't facilitate effective communication. In fact, they inhibit it.

At most offices, there is no Facebook equivalent; there's no set structure that's easy for employees to use and prohibits them from making changes that aren't in the best interests of users. As a result most companies' digital communications are like MySpace, with people adopting their own solutions with their own limited resources to do their jobs. Usually each department ends up creating its own little Web site or contributing its own page or portions of pages to the larger site. This model wasn't formed by design, but by accident of the fact that many parts of the company woke up around the same time and decided that digital communication was the key to their future success. True, some parts of a company may have strong talent and get it right; but most parts of the company have enthusiasm but not adequate resources or expertise, and the result is mediocre experiences and inconsistent, poor execution throughout the enterprise. And so we have chaos—a mess of jury-rigged technology and badly formatted, confusing presentations, Web sites, and employee portals—all of which preclude companies from effectively communicating to their constituents.

Realizing this problem, the most effective digital companies have developed internal software and organization solutions similar to what Facebook offers the world. I call this tactic concentric organization. Concentric organizations provide employees with a highly usable, tightly controlled, company-wide, centralized digital core. This infrastructure is

AUDIENCE

fig. 7

COMMUNICATORS

DIGITAL CORE

7. *Concentric Communication Layers*

then used by employees to communicate with their audiences. It can be thought of as three concentric circles.

- A central *digital core* is produced by user experience experts, engineers, and the oversight of top-level management. It's easy to use for nontechnical employees, and its design is tightly controlled and standardized to produce a consistent, highly usable experience for the external audiences receiving the information. It controls the infrastructure of the Web properties and digital communications. In Facebook parlance, one can think of the digital core as all the things that power Facebook. com: Facebook the company, its management, and armies of developers; its technology infrastructure; and its the Web site and overall user experience.

- A large, diverse group of *communicators* uses the digital core to reach their target audiences by posting information and communicating with the outside world. In the world of Facebook, communicators are all of its members who create profiles, share photos, and use the site as a tool to keep up with friends. In a business, communicators are employees.

- Finally, all of the information that's created by communicators is presented to the end *audience* in an easily digestible format. In the case of Facebook, the audience is the people who read the updates of friends from their news feed. For a company, the audience is its users—customers, prospects, and anyone else interacting with the organization in the digital space.

This strategy empowers employees, ensures a pleasant user experience, increases efficiency, and can become a company's competitive edge in the marketplace. What's even more important is that it requires limited digital talent in-house. One investment to pay for the talented designers, engineers, and managers to develop and operate a centralized system is all it takes. The rest of the company needs no specialized expertise.

This approach does sacrifice the individual choice and creativity of employees—no longer can a lone ranger throw up a Web page. But like Facebook, if the central system is well designed and enables the user to do what he or she wants to do more efficiently and effectively than before, most people will end up very appreciative of the new solution. The key to this approach is to think about employees as users as well—they're using the central infrastructure, to publish, transact, communicate, and do their jobs. And if the solution is as easy as uploading a video to YouTube, it has a real shot at getting adoption.

Done right, concentric organization offers several benefits for a company:

- **Economy of Scale:** With concentric organization, digital infrastructure is built once and used everywhere. As the central team adds more features or implements updates, they're instantly available to all users. The result is a tremendous economy of scale and cost savings.

- **No Redundancies:** Because things are built once and used everywhere, departments no longer need to redo or duplicate a tool that the core team built.

- **Agility:** The centralized team improves a company's ability to react nimbly to changes in the marketplace. The core digital group becomes a small, agile organization, and changes they make immediately improve the performance of the entire company. There's no more lumbering giant with seven different departments that need to weigh in before changes are made.

- **Empowers the Other Experts:** A sharp salesperson, a savvy marketer, a smart human resources staffer, a tactful customer-service agent, a PR expert—they all have strengths necessary to the success of the company and they all need to use digital technologies to be effective. But none are experts in technology. A strong, centralized infrastructure allows all of them to use digital technologies to improve their job performance, without any requisite expertise.

- **Resource Shortage Solved:** With digital talent centralized to the team that creates and manages the company-wide infrastructure, organizations need less digital talent than before, and the digital talent they do have is leveraged across as much of the company as possible. For example, an analytics expert can produce tools to let everyone in the company see meaningful data that can help them make decisions; there's no reason for separate analytics people and separate sets of analytics tools throughout the company.

CONCENTRIC ORGANIZATION IN ACTION

The Reader's Digest Association, founded in 1922, built a publishing empire on the back of a monthly magazine that featured curated, condensed articles, word games, and jokes. The magazine's U.S. circulation eventually hit more than seventeen million in the 1970s, and over time it extended to more than fifty countries. The company also publishes dozens of magazines outside of the Reader's Digest moniker as well as books, music, and videos. To power this global success, it developed the world's largest direct-mail marketing operation. But after decades of unparalleled performance, its fortunes started drying up. No print publisher was immune from the disruptive effects of the Internet.

In 2006, then president and CEO Eric Schrier directed his attention to driving revenue through digital media. A big move in that direction was the acquisition of Allrecipes.com, an online community for recipes and cooking. Then to complement this deep dive into the topic of food and to further establish digital media as a more significant source of income, Schrier fortified a centralized digital team of executives by empowering them to effect revenue-driving change across the organization—starting with the flagship ReadersDigest.com.

At the time, Reader's Digest's online operations were run like the MySpace model. There was no overarching digital strategy. About a dozen different groups of people were able to influence the content on the site. Design work was being done on a project-by-project basis without considering how it would support the brand or a sense of consistency or usability. Editors who paid attention to analytics didn't have enough influence to roll the insights into bigger-picture decisions. As a result, rather than reflect the brand or the interests of users, the site reflected the organization of the company. And the company wasn't organized to be a good Web site. By operating this way, user needs weren't being met—a real missed opportunity.

When the new members of the centralized team came in, they were tasked with the clear goal of running the U.S. Web site like a real business and increasing revenue from digital. Their chosen strategy: drive lots of traffic to the site to begin reaping revenue from ad sales as a start. This clear sense of purpose resulted in a structure through which they were able to evaluate all of the site's digital operations. It guided all decision making. The home page was now managed by the centralized team who took into account the company's business at large. A key piece of this focus was paying more attention to what users wanted. "Once you figure out what the user wants you have a real chance to make money off of it," says Lara Bashkoff, then vice president, strategy, of RDA Interactive. If the user hit a brick wall when he got to the site, it wouldn't matter how good the content was, he'd leave and not come back. So this team would apply laser-focused thinking. When someone wanted to update the site, the team asked themselves, would this update to the home page support a good user experience and ultimately increase revenue? The team then implemented a redesign that improved the look of the site to better reflect the quality of the brand and enhance usability. The success of this strategy and initiative gave the team the credibility to tackle bigger and more complex projects, such as Reader's Digest's international digital footprint.

At the time, the company's international Web sites spanned forty markets across South America, Australia, Canada, Mexico, Asia, and Europe, and every country had strikingly different Web presences. In some countries, online operations were fairly advanced, while in other regions, they had barely begun. Some markets had Web sites that primarily sold books. Others used the site for editorial purposes, but only updated the site once a month with the articles from the magazine. Others developed online-only articles and updated the site frequently. Some even sold wine and promoted branded credit cards, while others lived off traffic from sweepstakes. They were all doing what drove the most profit in their regions without any digital business structure from the top. Making this diverse group of sites usable and consistent with the Reader's Digest brand is when the real value of concentric organization came to light.

It wasn't going to be as easy as implementing the U.S. system across all of the other markets. For one, that would have been prohibitively expensive, and market by market, the site would have needed tweaking for operational and cultural differences. Nor would it be as simple as giving the international markets a static mock-up of the design with the expectation they'd build it into a Web site on their own. There had to be little to no room for misinterpretation and it should require little to no tech expertise. Bashkoff's team needed to develop a system that would form a healthy balance between taking overarching control and letting the individual markets run autonomously, a backbone that would empower the international employees to do their jobs better and with less strain while supporting the brand and profit generation globally.

The result was a "worldwide platform" consisting of an easy-to-apply standard design with some opportunity to tailor it to the local culture that would ensure brand consistency and usability. In addition, the centralized team built basic tools the individual markets could use to update their sites and tailor them to their individual needs. More advanced options were also offered to allow for greater customization for those markets that could afford to spend more on development. One of the most essential elements of the initiative was the introduction of a content management system, a piece of software that allows editors with minimal digital skills to simply slot text, headlines, and photos into an online form that then presents the content on the site in a consistent, universal format. This gave every market the power to publish text and photos online without compromising the site's design. What's more, the team constructed a digital library of years' worth of timeless and trusted published material from Reader's Digest, including recipes, jokes, health advice, and personal finance articles so the international markets had a full trough of content to draw from to complement what they were creating on their own. The result was a global presence that required little digital expertise or editorial staff, but could regularly publish articles and keep it all looking good.

In just over two years, the digital operations of Reader's Digest went from decentralized and unguided to a brand with a consistent content strategy and Web presence. Reader's Digest demonstrates the practical application of the concentric organization model.

- The **digital core** included behind-the-scenes technology and design. The team that creates and manages the digital core is akin to the Facebook employees who run Facebook.com.

- The **communicators** were the editors, writers, and country managers responsible for publishing Reader's Digest content.

- The **audience** are the individuals visiting ReadersDigest.com and reading articles.

PROGRESSIVE CENTRALIZATION

The Reader's Digest story also begins to illustrate a strategy I call progressive centralization. A key issue for implementing concentric organizational principles is deciding what to centralize when a company has many different departments, brands, and business units around the world, each with different interests. The solution is to centralize as much as possible that's common throughout the whole organization; then, building on this, centralize again based on what's common to a subset of the organization, and so on. In this manner, things are centralized as much as possible, until we reach the level of communication that is unique to an individual.

The principle of progressive centralization can be applied to all aspects of a company's digital footprint—not just its technology and Web site, but how Twitter and other social media are managed; how online customer service is handled; and how things such as analytics are managed throughout the enterprise. For all these areas, it's desirable to centralize what's common across brands and divisions, and let the things that are unique to a part of the company remain unique in the digital space. Done properly, this usually means centralizing most parts of the firm's digital footprint, while letting content, information, and digital branding remain distinct for each unit.

As a result, typical implementation of progressive centralization for companies managing several brands over several distinct markets looks as follows:

- Technology, interaction design, editorial standards, analytics, and social media infrastructure is centralized for the entire company.

- Visual design is standardized in accordance with each brand within the company, across all markets worldwide.

- Copy, promotions, information, and other editorial products are produced by the people most familiar with the respective information and need to directly publish it. These are typically managers associated with the specific brand and products on a country-specific basis. Content and promotions can be composed individually to drive performance; all of the infrastructure around the content is managed centrally.

Not all large conglomerates will be so receptive to an organization-wide effort to centralize digital communications. For example, a company hired HUGE to overhaul its global digital ecosystem, which at the time consisted of over one thousand distinct Web sites in countries around the world. This large company is just one part of a much larger organization, but the top level of the organization wouldn't buy in to a major restructuring of all their digital assets. This didn't mean that our partial standardization effort was a failure; it just wasn't as successful as it could have been. I urge eager user-centric managers to embrace pragmatism and standardize what they can. Any level of centralization is a big win.

EVOLVING TO CONCENTRIC ORGANIZATION

Even for subsidiaries of a larger whole, evolving to concentric organization—and in the process, becoming a user-first company—is a big shift. The transition typically happens in three phases:

- **Development:** A new Internet division is established to build digital capabilities in the organization. This is typically a separate, independent group that has the freedom to be nimble and effective.

- **Distribution:** Once the central team has developed a new digital design or product, it gets introduced for use to the larger organization in broad segments. In some cases to smooth transitions, digital experts can be distributed throughout the company. Often, from a profit-and-loss standpoint, online and offline are now merged—for example, all marketing has one balance sheet, all sales has another.

- **Integration:** In the final phase of the evolution, the new digital tools are fully integrated into the company. This doesn't just mean making sure every department is using the new tools; it means making sure that the online and offline functions of a particular area are combined to drive a user-first orientation throughout that part of the business. For example, a single customer-service group handles telephone, e-mail, and social media customer-service issues; and a retail merchandizing group handles products for the offline and online store. The result is an organization that's structured around the stage of the relationship between customer and business.

Distribution and integration require that the larger company—sometimes hundreds or thousands of employees, many of whom have worked in the same position for decades—change how it does things. Just as it can be hard to convince a parent company and its every arm to centralize, it can be trying to pry people from their comfortable roles.

This is the challenge that Sharon Rowlands, CEO of Penton Media, had to address when she evolved her business toward a model resembling concentric organization. As one of the largest independent business-to-business media companies in the United States, Penton publishes more than a hundred trade magazines targeted to thirty industries, everything from aviation to agriculture. And at the time, each magazine ran its own subpar Web site. She referred to the strategy as the "cowboy approach." Each had limited digital talent and resources, so they used shortcuts or not very good technology to meet their needs. The result was a bit of a mess, she said.

However, Penton couldn't afford to be bad at communicating through digital channels. As it had for the rest of the media industry, the

Internet had fundamentally challenged Penton's business model. "More companies are moving more of their marketing and advertising dollars to digital and away from print," says Rowlands, "and companies are looking to do more than just simply advertise for brand awareness. They're increasingly looking to get a return on investment on any sort of marketing investment and really specific results, particularly about lead generation for their companies. So Penton needed to really strengthen its digital capabilities and solutions in order to survive."

Rowlands decided to turn the traditional print publishing business into a "Web-first" media company. Her goal was to increase digital ad revenue from 15 percent to more than 50 percent of the pie—and she gave herself five years, until 2013, to make it happen. How'd she plan on doing it? With a centralized, highly usable digital infrastructure.

This would have been an incredibly challenging task even if every employee were game for the change. But her employees were likely to be more than just unsettled. They could potentially have become downright disgruntled. Not only were the individual business units accustomed to having the freedom to make their own decisions when it came to online communications, but much of the publishing company's staff were hard-core print media aficionados. "It was a hard change," she said, two years into the project. "A lot of the staff in media companies have grown up with magazines, they're very print-centric. It's definitely been very challenging to get them to embrace digital and what that means for editorial, because it's a whole different way of writing, it's a whole different way of thinking, it's a whole different deadline scenario to running a digital platform," she says.

The quickest way to lose the battle would have been to give them a digital solution that was hard to use and inflexible. "The reason a lot of central models fall down is that they're just not very good, so it creates a lot of frustration at the front end of the business," Rowlands says. "So what I've tried to do is hire very strong talent centrally and empower them to perform, so the businesses almost start saying, 'Wow, actually, that's amazing. Look what they did, they really responded to me.' It creates a kind of groundswell of support for the central resource."

Rowlands was right. Think about it: if it was hard to publish a photo to Facebook, nobody would be sharing photos. Similarly, companies cannot expect large numbers of employees to support the centralized digital system if it's too hard for them to use. And this is one of the most common reasons centralized digital efforts fail.

To drive support for the new system, beyond the usability of the system itself, she provided leadership, incentives, and clear direction to the company. This included a series of town halls and Webinars to reinforce the message that change had to occur in order for the company to survive and grow. Employees were also trained on how to write for a Web audience and how to use analytics to learn things like how many people are coming to the site, how long they're staying, and what they're reading most. In the end, though, no matter how enthusiastic the employees became about the new technology, they'd still likely revert to their old ways unless their pay and bonuses reflected the new responsibilities. In this case, salespeople were measured for pay increases and bonuses based on how much digital ad space they sold. Editorial employees were evaluated first on their willingness to participate in retraining. Later, their performances were measured by how they met digital objectives such as page views.

But even with all this plying, some people just can't make the shift. "I think the obstacle for management in leading this kind of change is to flush out your talent pool and to work out the people who can adapt and are willing to change and give them the opportunity, both the training and the tools, to make that change," Rowlands says. "But you also have to identify the people who can't make that change, and you have potentially to make very hard decisions, because you can't have a next-generation Web platform but not have the appropriate type of content to serve to your audience."

Looking at her progress, three components are vital to making the shift:

- **Leadership:** The centralized digital initiative must have top-down support. Everyone from the CEO to other high-level managers must communicate to everyone in the company what's happening and why it's important.

- **Money:** As Rowlands explains, "Don't shortcut it. You're talk-ing about building the foundation for a whole new business, and you don't really want to shortchange that and try to do it on the cheap and do it too quickly, because that will come back to bite you."

- **Talent:** Hiring the best digital talent possible is the best way to ensure a usable digital core that the company will appreciate rather than avoid using. It also demonstrates the company's willingness to support the initiative with resources, not just with words.

THE IMPORTANCE OF DIGITAL CORE EFFICACY

Stating the obvious, concentric organization only works if the digital core is effective. If the centralized solution fails to deliver, individual groups in the company will go off and do their own thing. Often, decentraliza-tion is the result of a failed centralization initiative. The center can lose its gravity in many ways: from being hard to use and badly designed, to being ill-supported by top-level management, to becoming a lumbering ineffective bureaucracy unable to keep up with the quickly evolving needs of the organization. Any weakness from the core is a window for entropic forces to return the company to the original model of decentral-ized digital activity. Indeed, there is no shortage of companies that started with a digital team back in the 1990s, only to disband the effort and let each group control its own destiny in the digital space. But as coordina-tion comes undone, as individuals within the organization splinter and begin to go around the system rather than through the system, the cha-otic "cowboy" results will likely spiral the company back to the land of MySpace, put the company at a competitive disadvantage, and risk the downfall of the entire organization.

This is similar to what happened to the Borders Group. In a little more than a decade it lost its profitable position in book retailing, lost hundreds of millions of dollars, and eventually entered bankruptcy. While the causes of Borders' demise were numerous, one major error was its ill-thought-out digital strategy marked by a poor digital core and a lack of focus on users.

Borders was plagued by technology problems from as early as 1995, starting with the company's inability to combine the computer and inventory systems of its Waldenbooks and Borders brand names. (This issue would end up unresolved.) Borders only began selling books online in 1998, three years after Amazon and a year after Barnes & Noble, and it had difficulty establishing a position in the marketplace. So in 2001, it asked Amazon for help, and entered into a partnership in which the online giant would develop and run its site. In effect, Borders outsourced its "digital core" to a competitor. This move proved to be disastrous. "I can see where it made sense on a spreadsheet, to give up the expense of running a site and just receive a portion of the profits," says Michael Norris, an analyst specializing in book retailing. "But the problem is that they created a disconnect between their online operation and their bricks-and-mortar operation." Beyond putting its digital operations into the hands of a chief competitor, the bricks-and-mortar retail and digital experiences became completely different, making it impossible to create a seamless multichannel shopping experience. This not only handicapped sales efforts but would have confused its customers. Seven years later, the company realized its mistake and took back control of its Web site. But by then it was hopelessly behind the curve. At the start of 2011, online hardcopy sales accounted for less than 3 percent of Borders' revenue—less than a third of what Barnes & Noble derived from its online hardcopy sales.

Borders' lack of emphasis on digital technology meant it also missed the e-book craze. Amazon began selling the Kindle in late 2007; Barnes & Noble followed with the Nook in late 2009; Apple released the iPad and launched its digital bookstore in spring 2010. But Borders' offering did not launch until June 2010, and the product—in partnership with Kobo, a Canadian manufacturer of e-readers—seemed more like a me-too product than a leader. In many ways, Kobo was Borders' last chance to catch up with its digitally savvy users; in the end, the company declared bankruptcy in February 2011.

I'm not claiming that Borders' lack of a strong digital core and user-first approach was the sole cause of its demise—indeed, the dramatic market shift in how consumers buy and consume books was a jarring reality for all of the players in the sector. But its inability to produce a timely and viable digital solution meant it was unable to meet present-day user needs.

ATTRACTING TALENT THAT CAN DELIVER

The stakes are high to create a digital core that can deliver on the user-first promise of a well-executed digital infrastructure. To build this infrastructure companies must attract and retain the right digital talent—ideally of the quality a true technology company could attract—and support them with an environment in which they'll be able to thrive.

Accomplishing this is no easy task. Demand is so high that the Internet's best talent can afford to be finicky. If they don't like where they're working, another firm with a more attractive salary and culture will quickly scoop them up. That could be your company. But it could just as easily be someone else scooping up your hard-won engineer or designer. To retain its staff and attract new achievers, Google has been known to offer unmatchable perks: free high-quality food, free laundry services, onsite car washes and oil changes for commuters, five thousand dollars toward the purchase of a hybrid, five hundred dollars in take-out food to ease your first four weeks at home with a new baby, onsite doctors, and dog-friendly offices. In 2010, Google even offered one talented engineer $3.5 million not to leave the company for Facebook. I know what you're thinking: "We're no Google, we can't compete with this." That may be true, but rest assured, there is a lot your company can do to attract the right people. Digital talent is eager for the chance to do great things, to make a real difference, to change the world. The promise of changing a giant, behind-the-times organization into an Internet-savvy business is an exciting challenge and a big way for ambitious people to make an impact. It can attract a lot of energy and enthusiasm from potential hires—but only if the company is serious about changing. If the business isn't committed, puts up too many hurdles, or doesn't give the digital staffers enough access, independence, and influence to make change, this will backfire.

To prevent this scenario, senior executives must proactively demonstrate the company's dedication to this digital transformation. There
must be a firm, well-communicated belief in the company's digital goals
and the significance of what the company is trying to accomplish—
starting with top management. Without this level of support, politics in
the organization or simply one influential disbeliever can hinder the effort and limit the extent of digital integration possible.

Leadership must also trust in the expertise of the digital team and
give its members authority over their own work. They can't be expected
to have every decision pored over by multiple layers of a bureaucracy.
Even if the rest of the company is managed by a command-and-control
style, the digital domain must be treated differently. In a technology
environment where new products and businesses spring up daily and a
new endeavor can go from conception to launch in a matter of months,
speed is essential. Reining in the momentum of the team members by
requiring them to wade through hours of meetings to get approval for
something will be read as inaction and a clear signal the company isn't
willing to grasp the new way of the world. Rather, the digital team must
have wide latitude for controlling the development and maintenance of
the digital foundation. It must be allowed to try out new ideas before
leadership is convinced they'll work. Accepting trial and error is important. It frees employees to take initiative and make decisions—and learn
from their mistakes. And it demonstrates an inspiring and attractive entrepreneurial spirit. Another way to create a fast-moving environment
like that of the technology industry is to organize the digital team into
small, nimble groups. This way they are able to quickly build and test
new ideas without having to gain whole-group consensus first.

The organization's physical environment is also of critical importance. The offices of most companies are often cold, impersonal places
with rows and rows of cubicles. These are places designed to run things;
in many cases they communicate power among certain individuals, but
they're certainly not designed for creative thinking and innovation.
What's required is an office environment that encourages the collabora-
tive ethos and speed intrinsic to the Web. Companies should do everything possible to make the group feel like a real digital company by

providing friendlier, open office space and perhaps even a location in a trendy young neighborhood. For example, when Johnson & Johnson decided to build up a unit that was oriented toward design and creativity, it allowed the new team to abandon the cubicle-filled New Jersey suburban office. The division planted a flag in an old industrial building in a trendy neighborhood in New York, with high ceilings and an office layout to match. If it weren't for J&J on the door, you'd think it was the next great startup . . . and the environment has the level of energy and excitement to match. These environmental choices may sound superficial, but quality of life is critical to fostering a digital media culture.

Providing the right growth opportunities is also critically important to building the right structure. It's likely that most of the digital team will be young—in their twenties and thirties—and they won't want to work in a hierarchical environment where it's structured to take a lifetime to get to the top. Career advancement for these folks should be based on merit. If they do a good job, they should be appropriately rewarded for it. Also their opportunities for advancement should extend beyond the ceiling of the digital department. They should see a clear path for uninhibited career development—if not, they won't see a reason to stay with the company in the long term. Of critical importance: can a digital executive manage a broader area of responsibility outside of the company's interactive footprint? Is there a user-first representative in the C-suite?

When all of these qualities come together, a big offline business is providing digital talent an offer that's hard to refuse: the culture of a technology start-up with the business know-how and financial support of an existing heavyweight.

A CULTURE OF GREATNESS

In all likelihood, the company you work for is great at something. That's why the organization is in business—it provides a certain product or service to a customer who is willing to pay for it, and it became great at this core dynamic, allowing it to grow and be successful. You may think your company is bad at a number of things, but look closely and you'll see it's probably pretty good at the core function that keeps the lights on. And it's so good at that one thing, it can get away with being mediocre in areas of its operations that aren't central to its success.

But now that your company is forced to run two "businesses"—the company's core operation and its digital footprint—greatness must triumph in both areas. A mediocre digital core will be rejected by both internal and external users. User-first companies must make digital great.

The notion of greatness must be core to the culture of your digital team members. Are they in your company for a job so they can pay the bills and be home at five to see the kids play soccer? Or are they driven to create a digital ecosystem for your business that's the best in the industry? The best cultures consist of talented and ambitious individuals who won't settle for okay work. Find the people who want to be pushed toward greatness. Promote a culture that prioritizes producing the best work possible, and recognize employees who deliver.

A culture of greatness includes one subtle component that is often missed in the world of innovation, and that's delivery. Our goal is not to create the *Mona Lisa*, the perfect work of art that will stand the test of time. It's to create the best user-first experience *on time* and with the resources available. As we'll discuss further in the next chapter, technology changes all the time; it's therefore reasonable to expect your company's digital infrastructure and user experience will continually evolve as well. The mantra is to launch things early and often, learn from what is live and how users react to it, and then make it better. There's no credit given to the perfect thing that never launches. So we must couple the will to innovate with a disciplined process that ensures all the trains run on time. That means starting small, launching small, and building from there. Focus on making the things that really matter to users; ignore everything else.

Beyond the right talent, passion, and a delivery orientation, the final piece to the greatness puzzle is money. Unfortunately, too many companies think about technology and the development of a digital core as a single event: we spend a lot of money, build the perfect thing, and we're done. This is often driven by the pragmatic reality that a large digital initiative was approved as part of a big capital expenditure budget, and since this budget is amortized over several years, there may not be a new pile of money to spend when the current budget is gone. This financial dynamic creates many problems in the digital arena. First, it creates tremendous pressure that the "big release"—the thing that launches as a result of the giant capital expenditure—is the perfect solution for the company. So managers work hard to squeeze in every feature they can think of, for fear that there won't be another chance to get their prized functionality into the product later on. And the release must be exciting enough to win the approval of senior management, who must justify this large, one-time expense. The result is that the launch gets bigger and bigger, adding risk to the project, and the date gets pushed out further. And once the launch finally happens, all the money is gone—no substantial budget for iterative improvements, learning from users, or evolving the experience in any way. The digital ecosystem is frozen in time, getting more and more outdated as the months pass. Fast forward a few years and the situation becomes dire enough for a complete overhaul, and the cycle repeats itself.

Avoid the budgeting trap. True greatness is about iteration, and the best digital initiatives have the financial support to continually evolve and build the experience. Say no to large capital investments and yes to continued, ongoing financial support.

INTERNAL START-UPS

A persistent challenge for organizations is defining the specific reporting structure for the central digital team. Are they part of marketing, information technology, or a separate division? In the end, whom they report to is less important than ensuring they're empowered by the executive suite to implement and enforce best-practice, user-first methodologies throughout the entire company. But sometimes they need to be even more independent. Some businesses looking to drive the right level of organizational change to their digital infrastructure embrace the notion of a start-up way beyond simply accommodating a start-up culture—they actually create internal start-ups. Rather than push through a company-wide digital transition, along the lines of what Rowlands accomplished with Penton, some CEOs conclude their companies are so entrenched in their old ways that the only way to change the company is to start a new one. They do this by creating a small, stealth group that reports directly to the CEO. This new group functions in the same way as a start-up would, free of the organization's potentially debilitating internal politics, management structure, and corporate culture. In relative isolation, the group imagines and creates the best possible new digital footprint. Once established, the rest of the company's digital efforts can then organize themselves around the new digital core.

Jeff Zucker, then CEO of NBC Universal, went the internal start-up route when creating Hulu, a popular Internet hub of old and new TV shows. In 2005, he watched the *Saturday Night Live* video short "Lazy Sunday"—which featured comedians Andy Samberg and Chris Parnell rapping about sleeping late, eating cupcakes, and watching the movie *Chronicles of Narnia*—go viral on YouTube, ultimately racking up millions of views. What was more stunning, fans had done this all on their own. They took the time to record the short, upload it, and share it with friends. NBC hadn't helped them do it at all. And then just a few months later, YouTube was sold to Google for $1.65 billion. "It seemed crazy to us," Zucker says. "That value was built principally on the back of our content." Zucker now realized NBC needed to control its online content and profit from it.

His initial effort was a company called NewCo—not Hulu. It was announced in March 2007 and meant to be a joint effort between Zucker and Peter Chernin, then president and chief operating officer of News Corp, which owns Fox. Together the powerful pair would devise a way to offer their television shows online. At the time they were leaps ahead of the competition. That same month, Viacom, the owner of MTV and Nickelodeon, took a different tack and went antidigital. It filed a $1 billion lawsuit against YouTube for posting its content without permission.

But rather than initially go the way of an internal start-up, NewCo started out with a traditional corporate product-development model where teams from NBC and Fox would get together to discuss their ideas on strategy and ideally make decisions. At one such meeting at a W hotel in Manhattan, more than one hundred employees from both companies assembled. The result "was a pileup of competing visions designed to protect existing turf," one Fox executive told *Fast Company*. The project was perceived to be foundering. Insiders at Google were even calling the project Clown Co. behind its back. To correct the situation, the two executives took a radical step: they hired Jason Kilar, a nearly decade-long Amazon executive who, among other accomplishments, led Amazon's entry into the DVD business, and they gave him nearly free rein over the enterprise.

Kilar's background was in retail and he made it clear he had completely different ideas about the project—he told the executives he envisioned it as a technology start-up, not an entertainment company. His goal would be to produce the winning product in just three months. To start, he cut loose almost all of the forty-five existing NewCo employees. This gave Kilar the space he needed to take some chances and make drastic changes.

To restaff the company, he went with what he called "the *Ocean's Eleven* approach." First he flew to China to buy a video start-up founded by a buddy and former Microsoft researcher. Then he handpicked additional staffers to form a small team composed largely of former Harvard Business School classmates, as well as Amazon and Microsoft veterans. He knew he needed people who had the talent and drive to reach the goal line in short order. And he found the right people. They saw the opportunity and came on board for this challenging gig, in spite of few corporate-style cushy perks. Kilar ran the business more like a garage-based startup than a big business enterprise. He scrapped his corner office for a work space more like a cubicle. No Google-like perks were available; no first-class tickets to distant business meetings. He told Charlie Rose cardboard boxes held up their computer monitors. The team's energy wasn't revved by dollars. They were attracted by the opportunity to make a difference and incentivized by equity stakes in the new company. Kilar named the company Hulu, a Chinese word that roughly translates to "holder of precious things."

In March 2008 the team launched the site. And within two months, the service had streamed an amazing sixty-three million videos. As Hulu grew, Kilar maintained a close eye on user experience, so much so that

Fortune magazine called it an obsession. He compulsively checked Twitter chatter about the company to monitor what users liked and disliked. The team combed through the site's analytics and then decisively acted on them. For example, after the team noticed that people were searching not only for individual shows but for broad categories such as "comedy" and "science fiction," it launched pages dedicated to those genres. To match the immediacy of the experience of watching TV in the traditional, remote control sense, Hulu minimized the time between someone clicking play and the video actually playing down to eight seconds. The site also responded to the market by giving users easy-to-use tools to embed the videos on their own Web sites. One of Hulu's breakthrough moments was how it reacted to Tina Fey's impression of Sarah Palin on *Saturday Night Live.* Within a day after the live broadcast, the team posted the clips—cashing in on the immediate "you-have-to-see-this" chatter. The videos were viral sensations, and Hulu was on an unbeatable trajectory. In 2009, Disney, which owns ABC, joined the initiative. By the end of the year, the site boasted forty-three million unique visitors a month. Six months later competitor Viacom lost the $1 billion suit it had filed against YouTube. Zucker and Chernin could finally revel in their success.

Hulu could never have developed as quickly or successfully as it did under the direct leadership of traditional television executives tasked with managing hundred-year-old media companies. They were too set in their ways, too protective of existing structures, too limiting. By embracing the internal start-up model, NBC and Fox essentially invented what is likely to be the model for online television viewing for years to come. The distance from its parent companies allowed Hulu to attract the type of talent and allow for the user-centric management that every business needs to thrive in the digital space.

MAKING THE TRANSITION

Transitioning to concentric organization is a huge undertaking. It can't be realized without building a strong digital core; this digital core can't be built without the right talent; the right talent need to realize freedoms potentially nonexistent in the rest of the company; and then the solution needs to be user-first enough that the rest of the company eagerly adopts the change. With this solid foundation in place, it'll be much easier to evolve the company's product mix, marketing, sales, and customer-service efforts to be user-first.

One element of this foundation we haven't yet discussed is the actual technology behind it. Concentric organization empowers the people in the company to produce best-in-class, digital media solutions. But if the technological infrastructure of the larger business isn't up to par or the company is unwilling to replace its existing systems, all of these efforts could be a complete waste of time. Technological barriers can stifle the best intended digital core. What's required is a commitment to disposable technology, the subject of the next chapter.

CHAPTER SUMMARY: CONCENTRIC ORGANIZATION

Market Insights

- Organizations are faced with a chronic shortage of digital talent. The lack of an adequate labor pool forces companies to be creative in how they embrace Internet technologies. To compound matters, the specific skill sets required for implementing a user-first strategy (for example, specialized design and technology expertise) are even more scarce.

- Companies also suffer from a mismatch of talent—for example, executives forced to be designers—that is the result of insufficient technical infrastructure provided by the company—and often, misguided employee enthusiasm.

- Many elements key to the creation of the digital core are fixed-cost investments. As a result, cost requirements are generally independent of the number of users or size of audience the initiative reaches. The larger the effect of the digital investment, the less it costs, so to speak. It pays to truly embrace concentric organization.

Strategic Imperatives

- Companies are able to efficiently implement a user-first strategy through concentric organization. This is an organizational structure that centralizes all digital activities, creating a simple, easy-to-use platform that allows interactive media to be broadly used throughout the organization. This approach is similar to Facebook itself: a central core group of people (Facebook, the company), creates a standard and tightly controlled platform (Facebook, the Web site), that allows lots of people to easily publish and communicate with a broader audience. The result is a system that achieves economies of scales and enforces user-centric guidelines throughout the entire organization, regardless of an individual employee's digital competency.

- The central digital team can be part of any department or its own division—what matters is it has the support of the top-level management to build and implement user-first solutions throughout the entire company. The team must be empowered by leadership to make change, have the technology to deliver (more information in the next chapter), and enough resources to properly handle execution. Without the right combination of leadership, talent, and resources, the central digital core risks failure—jeopardizing the entire organization.

- From a personnel standpoint, the central team must be as good as the best Internet companies—after all, they're managing the organization's "software layer" that fosters all interaction with users. This often means the company must embrace a culture and mentality more representative of a start-up or technology company to attract the best and brightest. In many cases, companies make this happen by creating a new, internal start-up that's outside of (and protected from) the conventional management structure, which ensures they have the freedom and culture to succeed.

- Progressive centralization is an important model for implementing concentric organization on a large scale. With this approach, one finds the components of digital communication that can be centralized across the broadest set of the company's operations, and then works downward, centralizing things as much as possible for different parts of the company, until reaching a point where communication must be unique.

3

Disposable Technology

Bring the Strategy to Life by Constantly Changing, Revising, and Throwing Away Software

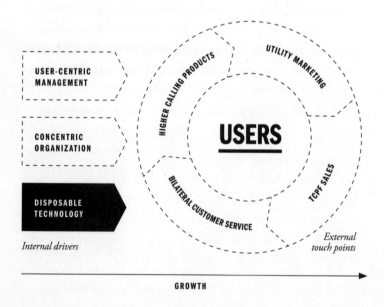

The digital core, discussed in chapter 2, must be powered by technology that's designed to meet user needs. But this means more than a piece of software being easy to use by internal constituents who have limited tech expertise. And it's more than a well-designed, usable experience with which external users enjoy interacting. To meet both of these objectives, the technology powering all user experiences must be incredibly agile, so it can be quickly tweaked and changed to meet rapid advancements in user trends and business needs. Failure to commit to a foundation of nimble user-centric technology is *the* fatal flaw that can take down otherwise unsinkable businesses, leaving gaping holes for competitors to fill. The demise of Blockbuster Video demonstrates this principle.

When the doors opened to the first Blockbuster Video at the edge of a strip mall in Dallas, Texas, on October 19, 1985, so many people turned up the line went out the door. It had more movies than any regular mom-and-pop shop—an unprecedented eight thousand family friendly titles on the dominant technology, VHS. Already 28 percent of all U.S. households had a VCR, and Blockbuster was there to give this living room staple more value. The chain also used state-of-the-art technology to realize as yet unseen efficiencies. It set up a snazzy computer system that used bar code scanners to quickly read key information from member cards and the movies they were renting or returning. At the start, Blockbuster's use of technology was synced with user desires and streamlined business processes.

But a funny thing happened on the way to the new millennium—technology used by customers and companies rapidly evolved, and not just from VHS to DVD. In 1998, Blockbuster got its first glimpse of digital competition when Netflix, then a little start-up, placed its first red envelope in the mail.

Netflix, as we all know, was more than an unthreatening newcomer. As of March 2011, it could boast an $11 billion market cap. Looking back at its last thirteen years, we can see how it used technology to nimbly improve its operations and strengthen its relationship with users. Without the limitations of retail locations and limited shelf space, Netflix could stock more movies than Blockbuster and didn't have to resort to late fees to keep enough movies in stock. It gave users a tool to maintain their own queue of movies to order, so they didn't have to stand in a store wondering, "What was it I wanted to see next?" It offered subscribers spot-on, personalized film recommendations and reached out to the wider developer community for ways to improve its algorithm. As social networking took center stage, Netflix tried its hand at building its own social network. This initiative ended abruptly, but the company still took advantage of the technology enough to attract 1.2 million Facebook fans. It then broke new ground by streaming video to dozens of devices including personal computers, smart phones, and gaming consoles. To power its back end, it relied on the flexibility of cloud-based Amazon Web Services, so it could scale its operations quickly when needed. Netflix embraced the notion of constant technological evolution and improvement.

Blockbuster, on the other hand, did not. It approached the change in technology with a slower, conservative, big-business approach. In July 2000, with an eye toward the future, Blockbuster announced a plan to offer on-demand streaming videos to its customers over the Internet (at the time through DSL only). But the service couldn't get off the ground. Rather than build the system internally or partner with a start-up (Netflix asked Blockbuster for a partnership deal in 2000 but Blockbuster turned them down), Blockbuster picked the soon-to-implode-in-disgrace Enron as its *twenty-year* technology partner for the initiative. In 2009, two years after Netflix, Blockbuster finally launched its own streaming video service. Its technology, however, was inferior: movies weren't accessible through Macs, iPhones, iPads, or gaming consoles.

Technology was Blockbuster's Achilles' heel, and efforts to solve this problem proved problematic. In 2007, the chain hired a new CEO, formerly of 7-Eleven, and he brought along his chief information officer. When they walked in, they discovered Blockbuster was still using early 1990s technology, such as IBM minicomputers, and virtually all departments were separated from each other by technology limitations. They recognized this was bad. But again they went with a heavy-handed solution. To help update and streamline the system, the new leader set up a team of *two hundred* technologists in India.

I could continue discussing Blockbuster's failed attempts to rival Netflix in the rent-by-mail category and compete with Redbox's increasingly prevalent DVD-rental kiosks. Both efforts are rife with management and technology misfires. But you get the picture. Blockbuster filed for bankruptcy in 2010. In spite of having the strategic vision to know it had to adjust, it was a victim of its own technological inability. The result could have been different had Blockbuster invested in solutions that would allow for rapid change. Netflix understood the future, and that future is constant change, which means systems are needed to allow for evolution. You have to be able to throw things away, start again, and modify things. You have to have a disposable mindset.

I use the term "disposable technology" for solutions that are easy to launch, maintain, update, and get rid of if necessary. This is the critical third driver of the user-first company. User-centric management defines the vision and leadership. Concentric organization is the corporate structure needed to succeed, and the right technology, disposable technology, is the critical executional piece that brings the strategy to life.

The concept of disposable technology is simple. Given the rapid pace of change in technology trends and user behaviors, companies—even huge multinationals—must learn to rely on lightweight solutions that can easily be manipulated, installed, and uninstalled. It's the antithesis of twenty-year contracts with other stodgy multinationals and an outsourced team of two hundred developers; it's the only way companies can move quickly enough to keep pace with the rapid evolution of user behavior. Technologies that fit the paradigm of disposable technology are generally marked by six key attributes: replaceability, controlled interoperability, maintainability, updateability, eventual scalability, and speed.

REPLACEABILITY

A technology can be considered disposable if you can fix its parts without replacing the whole. It's like a car. If it needs a new fan belt, you don't replace the whole vehicle. You replace only the broken piece, in this case the fan belt. If your car needs new tires, again you don't replace the whole vehicle. Rather you buy a new set of tires, and maybe they're even better quality than your old ones.

The same goes for software. It should be designed so that any individual element is easy to replace or upgrade. In practice, this means the architecture of the software should be *modular*, so any one "module" can be swapped out without requiring the whole system to change.

Drupal, a content management system (CMS), is a great example of a disposable technology. (A content management system is a Web-based program that manages all of the content a company publishes to its Web site. It often has fields similar to those you might fill out when making your Facebook profile or entering information into an online job application.) Drupal is available for free download by anyone—individual blogger or multinational company—and offers Webmasters more than eight thousand different modules to use on their sites. They can use them to add a chat room games, e-commerce functionalities, display ads from Google Adsense, multilingual Web page translation, and much, much more. Developers can also build their own modules for use in the system. And all of it is easy to install, customize, or delete from a page.

In 2009, the Miami Dolphins football team redesigned its Web site using Drupal's modular infrastructure. The team's goal was one any major brand would identify with: to better engage its users and integrate more modern technologies such as social media onto the site. To accomplish its objective, the Dolphins' tech team installed Drupal, understanding that its free price tag didn't preclude it from being enterprise-strength software. They clearly knew this kind of democratized solution would allow them to keep up with the rapidly evolving trends in digital technology, to interact with their fans, and deliver content to them in the most cutting-edge, popular ways possible. At the end of the redesign project, the Dolphins ended up fitting together more than seventy modules, both custom designed and preexisting. The final site, which hosts about a million visits on game day, boasts live statistics feeds, video for events such as press conferences and player interviews, a large photo gallery, advertising banners, and bilingual content. It's a site any user-centric manager could be proud of.

CONTROLLED INTEROPERABILITY

A technology can be considered disposable if it is able to interact not just with users, but with the technology behind other systems—be it other

Web sites, applications, or internal systems. This opens the door for warp-speed evolution because it allows the company to easily integrate new technology, to integrate itself into the technology of others, and at its most open, allow third-party developers to use the system to power their own individual solutions.

In practice, this often means a strategically chosen portion of a company's technology should be designed to share information with other systems either outside or inside the company. People in the tech industry call this an API, which stands for application programming interface. It's literally a user interface for other programs, rather than human users. You see the results of APIs nearly every time you go online. Many technology and media companies use APIs to superpower their technical teams and syndicate their content around the globe at no charge. For example, you know how nearly every company Web site you go to has a Google Map showing where it's located? That's made possible by the Google Maps API, a portion of Google Maps code that allows any Webmaster to embed Google Maps into his or her own site. As of June 2010, developers had used it to embed maps onto 350,000 different Web sites. Twitter's API has also helped drive the service into ubiquity. With the ability to access some of Twitter's functionality, independent programmers have been able to build Twitter-based services and programs—many of which are more elegant and usable than Twitter itself. These uses of Twitter's technology that exist outside of Twitter.com actually drive three-quarters of Twitter's traffic. Company cofounder Biz Stone has called the release of its API, "the most important thing we've done." Then there's National Public Radio. Its API lets developers link to more than 250,000 of NPR's programs dating from 1995. Literally anyone, from an individual blogger to a large radio station, can easily embed NPR stories into their sites. It's also allowed NPR fan and professional developer Bradley Flubacher to develop a free iPhone app—"NPR Addict"—that lets users search and stream thousands of podcasts of shows such as *This American Life* and *Morning Edition* to their devices. More than one billion NPR stories have been delivered via its API in a single month. In an era when most media organizations are faltering because of the digital revolution, NPR's decision to release an API has helped it become more widespread and influential.

Of course, it is not in a company's best interest to share all of its information. Before deciding if your company should release some of its information or technology via an API, you must distinguish between what is truly proprietary and what information would be valuable on the open market. Facebook is an excellent example of this—while its API allows Facebook to be embedded in nearly every site in existence, it's not possible to use Facebook APIs to export one's contact list. While many people complain about this policy, it's strategically sound. It is only letting developers use Facebook's functionality and data in ways that will strengthen its position in the marketplace. Facebook, and any other company, can only remain competitive if it strategically *controls interoperability* to its advantage.

MAINTAINABILITY

To be considered disposable technology, software must be easy to maintain, upgrade, and customize as necessary. As a rule, it's unwise for a company to rely on software if its in-house team is incapable of maintaining, updating, and changing it on its own. Being dependent on outside providers can make it difficult for a business to implement simple updates. And over time, if key software isn't maintained, the company can lose ground in the race for digital leadership.

The easiest way for companies to get hog-tied by hard-to-maintain systems is if they become enamored with dreams sold by convincing technology salespeople. While charismatically presented PowerPoint slides showcasing all of a system's strengths may persuade, these types of partnerships can result in technical solutions that are either proprietary to the provider or too complex to be maintained in-house. A few years ago, one of our multinational clients hired a technology vendor to revamp its Web presence. The contracting vendor installed a proprietary e-commerce system that used all of its own technology. Everyone at the company was happy with the solution . . . until they wanted to make changes. For every minor update, the firm had to go through the external provider and pay a giant bill. The company was trapped with an incredibly expensive and yet completely frozen site. To rectify the situation, the company had to bite the bullet: let go of its fancy system and switch to a more open one that could easily be maintained by the company's internal team.

Another way to end up with an unmaintainable system is by agreeing to develop software in a language that your own team isn't familiar with. When a group of developers gets together to discuss a new initiative, one of the most painfully drawn-out conversations will be what language to use. What are the relative merits of .NET, PHP, Ruby on Rails, Node.js, or other programming flavors of the month? And within each programming language, debates continue about different software packages, components of technology stacks, and so forth.

In the end, most programming languages and technologies can meet many different needs. You want to rule out the ones that won't work, but there is usually more than one right choice. After that, it's simply a matter of choosing a technology that matches the skill set of existing employees or easy-to-hire staff. Next time you're involved in a quasi-religious, unwinnable battle about the best technology to use, focus instead on what technologies will be easiest for your organization to manage. All the functionality in the world can end up being a nightmare if you have to contract with another firm every time you want to make changes to your Web site.

UPDATEABILITY

Consumers expect Web sites to have the latest information, newest promotions, up-to-date job listings, relevant staff bios, most recent press releases, timely investor relations materials, and so on. The creation of this content is the responsibility of dozens if not hundreds of employees—and, as we discussed in the last chapter, not all of them are especially tech-savvy. This brings us to one of the most important attributes of a disposable technology solution: updateability. Just as software needs to be easily maintained, updated, and managed, the software itself must allow the site's content to be changed frequently and with ease.

But this isn't the case at many companies. Often, businesses are hamstrung by software that requires technical expertise, laborious and time-intensive steps, or worse still, a third party to make content changes. This is a recipe for disaster. Because if the employees have trouble quickly updating text, photos, or other information, then information will not get updated, resulting in a less-than-desirable digital experience available to the outside world.

The simplest way to ensure easy publishing is to have a well-designed content management system, or CMS, in place. Again, it's basically software that makes it easy for non-technical personnel to change content on a Web site, whether it's adjusting text or changing a photo. But be forewarned, not all CMSs are created equal. Some are harder to use than others and some have been designed with specific purposes in mind. Test the software yourself—it should be so easy to update content that everyone wants to do it—just like Facebook makes it easy for people to update their profile. Companies must think beyond the cursory "we need a CMS" and choose one that best fits the end-use of the system and the capabilities of the employees.

Access to analytics is another key aspect of updateability. As discussed in the first chapter in reference to JetBlue's Web site optimization and in the second chapter about Google's school of iterative design, analytics are the anonymous digital footprints left by your site's visitors that show where they click, what page they enter the site from (such as Google), what page of your site they leave from, how long they're on your site, what geographic location they're in, if it's an e-commerce site how they shop and how they proceed through the checkout process, and more. This information can be used to identify ways to improve a site's usability. For instance, if a Webmaster of an e-commerce site notices that visitors are abandoning the site after putting an item in their "cart," the engineer knows to investigate what problems users may be having in the checkout process. But unless there's a system in place to present this data in an easy-to-read way through a dashboard of charts and graphs, it's nearly unusable. One of these systems is mandatory if the site is going to be well maintained and updated. In the best-case scenario, the service providing the analytics dashboard will also offer live testing of different promotions, copy, and creative treatments—and of course these tests should be able to be launched and updated quickly and without the help of engineers.

EVENTUAL SCALABILITY

Any company that launches a digital initiative today has to anticipate that it will be used by millions of people, if not more. Technologies put in place without scalability in mind are apt to come crashing down by soaring demand.

This was exactly what tanked the old social networking site Friendster, a precursor to Facebook. At its start, Friendster had a bright future. Early adopters were using it en masse to connect with their friends and acquaintances. But the more people who joined, the slower the service became. (Company leadership focused more intently on expanding than on building a system that could withstand the expansion.) Users were waiting a full forty seconds for a page to load. As Jim Scheinman, a former Friendster executive said: "It basically came down to failed execution on the technology side—we had millions of Friendster members begging us to get the site working faster so they could log in and spend hours social networking with their friends. I remember coming in to the office for months reading thousands of customer-service e-mails telling us that if we didn't get our site working better soon, they'd be 'forced to join' a new social networking site that had just launched called MySpace . . . the rest is history."

Friendster didn't err in not being scalable; in the beginning nothing is truly scalable the way it needs to be. Its mistake was failing to focus on a clear path to eventual scalability once its user base started to grow.

Companies often run into trouble by spending too much money up front on engineering the initial product to make sure it's scalable from the get-go. But this doesn't work because developers can't predict how real people are going to use their products. This makes it incredibly risky to secure scalable solutions for particular, planned bottlenecks before launch.

The best approach is to assume the system will eventually have to host a very large number of users, and to have a general idea of how you'd evolve the system over time so it would scale—but don't put in the work right away. Instead, launch a user-first experience quickly without worrying too much about scalability in the short term. Figure out what connects and resonates with users, and once real usage patterns are established, then spend engineering time scaling the system as it becomes clearer what the true bottlenecks are. This approach is why Twitter's functionality and appearance didn't change much for the first few years. Engineers had to spend every last resource just keeping the system up and running to support the billions of messages running through it before focusing on beautifying the interface.

Scalability was also a big issue for blogging site Tumblr. It launched in 2007 and 75,000 bloggers switched to the site nearly immediately. But by July 2010, it had more than 6 million users and was adding another 25,000 every day. The rapid growth in traffic began leading to service disruptions and finally, in December 2010, to a 24-hour period where the service completely crashed. In a public apology, Tumblr staff admitted its rapid increase in popularity had compromised the site's usability. "While you might feel like you've gotten used to seeing errors on Tumblr recently, know that this is absolutely unacceptable to our team," the company wrote. "We are determined and focused on bringing our infrastructure well ahead of capacity as quickly as possible. We've nearly quadrupled our engineering team this month alone, and continue to distribute and enhance our architecture to be more resilient to failures like today's."

SPEED

Speed is one of the most important components of a good user-first experience. The back button is only a click away, and users are notoriously fickle when it comes to speed. Users want instant gratification, and that means having pages appear right away, as soon as they click. The moment they see a spinning "loading" icon, or a blank page with the browser furiously trying to load content, it's over—users leave. This isn't just a subjective determination; it's been demonstrated with analytics. For example, for every hundred milliseconds that Amazon can speed up the time it takes for its pages to load, it gains a 1 percent increase in revenue. The Aberdeen Group similarly did a study that showed page views decline 11% for every extra second it takes for a Web page to load.

From a technology standpoint, this means it's critical to design a system where responsiveness—raw speed—is of primary importance. And like all other aspects of disposable technology, this isn't a one-shot deal, it's an ongoing quest: how can we make things faster? Where are the bottlenecks that make things slow, and what can we do to improve them? By iteratively focusing on speed, technology becomes responsive to user needs—and software gets continually streamlined and improved over time.

TRANSITIONING TO DISPOSABLE TECHNOLOGY

President Barack Obama and his administration's digital team are dedicated to disposable technology. After Obama was inaugurated in January 2009, his new media team flipped the switch on a total, disposable technology redesign of Whitehouse.gov—the digital flagship of the presidential brand.

Like many businesses considering digital change, the team had to revitalize an old site. In this case it was George W. Bush's version of Whitehouse.gov. It was functional, but it showed signs of age—a dated design, unfriendly navigation, a relatively inflexible back end, and few Web 2.0 tools that citizens could use to interact with the administration. Obama's team not only wanted to create a fresh look with new graphics and information architecture, it wanted to build a site that would engage visitors, as well as embody and promote the president's values of communication, transparency, and participation. "[We were] looking at how we can help the White House amplify the president's message and get our content out as technology changes how and where people consume information," said Macon Phillips, Obama's new media director. This meant utilizing a blog, slide shows, videos, live video streams presented with real-time discussions of events on Facebook, podcasts of Obama's weekly address, various newsletters—and also being ready to adopt whatever tech advances were sure to come during Obama's term in office.

To accomplish this ambitious, user-centric goal, instead of installing a large, monolithic system meant to serve one set of predetermined technology needs, the new media team worked with the White House's existing technology partners to develop an infrastructure based on Drupal. This decision defined the tone, speed, and achievable goals of the development process. David Cole, at the time a senior adviser to the president's chief information officer, said the team could have spent late nights reinventing the wheel and building all of the functionalities it wanted from scratch. Instead it only had to build a few custom modules and apply the best of the existing modules in a way that was most appropriate for its business needs. With much of the site's tools predesigned, the team could focus its expertise on more complex challenges. "A lot of the custom development that we did surrounded scalability," says Cole. "We wanted to make sure we could handle national events that were going on and really be prepared for anything." One key objective was to make sure pages could refresh quickly and automatically as users input new content. The team also had to address issues surrounding security; it is the White House's site after all.

When the site launched on January 20, 2009, improvements and updates were to occur consistently. The team still had sixty or so more features they were interested in implementing. This meant the in-house staff and the contracted external team would likely continue to maintain an agile, short development cycle to allow for iterative improvements—a clear sign of a dedication to disposable technology.

The use of plug-and-play, open-source software raised some eyebrows in the community—disposable technology is often more closely associated with small-time sites that can't afford fancy proprietary tools than with a body as buttoned-up and large scale as the White House. But the model implemented by Obama's team has since been embraced by several other government agencies including the Federal Communications Commission and the Department of Commerce. "By building the site internally and using open-source technology that doesn't require expensive software licenses, we now have a site that looks and performs better than our previous site," said T. Neil Sroka, the Department of Commerce's director of new media at the time of the May 2010 launch. "We have developed resources that will help us efficiently build other visually modern, technologically advanced Web sites in the months and years to come."

CHOOSING THE RIGHT TECHNOLOGY LEADERSHIP

Given the importance of technology in the execution of a user-first site, a business committed to success must have a qualified technologist near the helm. Without the expertise of this instrumental player, it's very possible the ambitions of the user-centric manager and team will never come to fruition.

Early in my career, I launched an e-mail greetings Web site. At the time, I didn't have the skills to build it myself so I hired a few people who I thought could make it happen. For a brief period in the mid-nineties, the site was the third-largest in its market in terms of traffic and one of the five hundred largest sites on the Web. But our technology was terrible, and the more popular we became, the more our site crashed. We were trapped, unable to grow at the very moment everyone wanted to send e-greeting cards. It took us six months to correct the problem, and by then Blue Mountain Arts steamrolled forward to dominate the space. Eventually Blue Mountain sold for $780 million, and my site faded away. That type of blunder is common. So common, many venture capitalists won't invest in businesses that aren't run by tech people. Without someone who understands technology in the lead, it's often unclear if the promised products can actually get built. After my six-month debacle, I decided to become a good programmer—if only to be sure I could evaluate the right technology and talent myself.

But few executives have the luxury to learn programming in their spare time, so most executives are forced to hire the chief technology officer by taking a leap of faith. To make that leap of faith less scary, executives should focus on hiring a technologist with a distinct user-first approach—someone who cares about designing digital experiences that are pleasurable to use. They should find someone who:

- **Speaks their language.** Just because a job contender uses fancy tech lingo during the interview doesn't mean she's going to be a good technology leader. The right candidate should talk more about the philosophy of disposable technology and the importance of superior end-user experiences than specific software platforms or server configurations. Companies that succeed in the digital space by focusing on the user have engineering personnel who share this vision.

- **Has overseen digital projects that provide great user experiences.** This is the baseline qualification for any potential hire for a tech-leadership position—he or she should have a record of making products with great usability. This is the easiest way to evaluate the person. If he doesn't have anything like that to show you, don't hire him.

OVERCOMING THE BARRIERS TO GREATNESS

Great technology leaders must be able to transcend organizational and cultural barriers to make real user-first experiences come to life. One barrier is reliance on the IT department. Information technology departments are typically structured to manage, not build things. They are set up to maintain the company's technology infrastructure—things such as e-mail, security, desktop computers—not for designing and implementing innovative user-facing digital experiences. But often they're asked to build experiences, because they're the only technology folks in the organization. Some IT departments relish the expansion of responsibility, but others reluctantly take on the task, because they know they're not the ones who should be doing this kind of work. To rise above this contentious issue, the technology leader must build his or her own team. But it needs to be done with great care. Anyone with a background in building Web sites isn't enough.

The traditional career path of a software engineer disincentivizes the creation of user-first systems. Often, the more senior you are, the less time you spend writing the code that creates the look and feel of the site. As a result, software engineers intent on advancing their careers do everything possible to leapfrog past front-end design and create complex back end systems. This often leaves junior engineers to create the user interface, largely the determining factor for the organization's success in digital media. And it's rare for an engineer to also be a great designer or professional communicator. The result often ends up being software that meets a set of defined technological requirements, but not software that is easy to use or in any way beautiful—or on brand. But engineers often end up designing the front-end experience anyway, because nobody else has designed it, and the product has to get quickly coded and launched. Even in the most sophisticated professional services firms that build software for the Fortune 500—companies such as Accenture or IBM—good interface design is often not a core part of the process.

To overcome this cultural issue at your company, the chief technologist must try to find strong engineers who care about users and couple them with experienced user-interface designers. Yes, there are professional user-interface designers. Hire them. They have high-tech know-how and a strong sense of design and usability. By creating a team that cares about users, the old barriers to great design can start to fade away. Fortunately, the start-up world is making this easier to achieve—every story of a beautiful, simple product that becomes massively successful is more motivation for the development community to care about user experience.

THE POWER OF MICROTEAMS

The new user-first technology team doesn't have to be big. When we think about building software, it's easy to picture an army of developers (maybe outsourced to India?) working long into the night, coding away. That's the old model. The wide availability of open-source software as well as third-party APIs and services have radically cut the time required to bring products to market. This means you don't need big teams spending months starting from scratch. Today it's more effective to have a small digital core of experts working to create customized best-in-class solutions. If the initiative is big enough, then it's best to create a series of small teams that operate independently on discrete tasks. Each of these components then can be treated as separate pieces of the same puzzle that will fit together to form a full, robust ecosystem. Other advantages of the microteam organizational structure: it complements a more agile, consistent development cycle, one of short sprints rather than long hauls, where new or existing components are regularly updated, released, and tested with actual users. It also minimizes the risk of sprawling, over-budget, late projects because there isn't one monster project to control, just small pieces of the project to manage. And it keeps the lean, entrepreneurial spirit alive in your tech teams, because they maintain a degree of autonomy. Really small teams are a win-win situation.

This organizational structure has powered some of the greatest digital successes. Twitter co-founders Jack Dorsey and Biz Stone built a Twitter prototype in two weeks. "Instapaper," the massively popular app that lets you bookmark articles in your Web browser and then seamlessly loads them onto your iPad, iPhone, or Kindle, was created by developer Marco Arment in his spare time. Even Facebook's five hundred developers work in small teams of three to five on short assignments that usually last no longer than a month or two. "We don't have the layers of management approval. We don't pass things up and down the chain. The team working on the product development makes the decisions," says Mike Schroepfer, Facebook's vice president of engineering. "People are pushing new features and code to the site every day. It's really about trying to remove barriers and reduce friction in development."

Facebook, Twitter, and Instapaper are all testaments to the adage that each additional developer is exponentially less productive than the previous one. It's a case of diminishing returns: each warm body only adds to the time required for coordination, communication, and oversight. The more layers of management and the more people who need to come to consensus about the viability and quality of a new component, the fewer new innovations your site will release to the market and the slower your development process will become. To truly take advantage of disposable technologies, the tech team behind the effort needs to be empowered to build and employ site improvements as quickly as possible, to keep pace with the evolution of digital technologies and user expectations.

Today, advancements in technology are happening so quickly that it's risky to spend big on any solution (including a new tech team) that's not set up to rapidly react to advancements in the marketplace. Even consumers are having this problem. As of early 2011, Digital Leadership Set member Best Buy started offering TV buyers an "obsolescence protection plan" that offers customers as much as 50 percent off when they upgrade to a new model, depending on the amount of time that has passed. This however is not a problem that's going to go away. It's key that a company set up its own "obsolescence" insurance by using disposable technology to power its concentric organization and user-centric management. Only once all three internal drivers are in sync can they be leveraged to make a real impact on the organization's touch points with the external world. In the next chapter, we'll discuss the first of the external touch points: higher calling products, a clear way to demonstrate your user-first mindset through your firm's actual product mix.

CHAPTER SUMMARY: DISPOSABLE TECHNOLOGY

Market Insights

- The primary reason companies fail to become user-first is an inability to execute from a technology standpoint. Technology initiatives typically fail because they can't evolve over time, and quality is sacrificed to match an organization's existing, inadequate technology infrastructure.

- Given the rapid change of information technology—a rate of change that is increasing over time—technology obsolescence within an organization is a high and growing risk.

Strategic Imperatives

- Companies best manage technology by building solutions that embrace the notion of "disposable" technology—the idea that technology will continually change, evolve, and be replaced over time. While commitment to technology to drive business is a long-term focus, most of the actual technology investments should be short term and ephemeral. This is in sharp contrast to the once commonplace practice of implementing a large technology platform that must last for years. The result is a degree of nimbleness that allows companies to continually adjust their technology to changing market environments and user needs.

- The best disposable technologies are those that are built so that any single component of the solution can be replaceable with newer technology as needed; can eventually scale (through further investment or development) to support large numbers of users; is easily maintainable; and can be simply updated. Finally, disposable technologies should be built for speed and rapid response time, the most critical driver to user satisfaction.

- From an organizational standpoint, effective disposable technologies are typically built with small, nimble teams run by a technology leader who is passionate about creating highly usable experiences. The model of armies of offshore coders creating big lumbering systems is a thing of the past.

4

Higher-Calling Products

Create Digital Services That Make Your Products More Valuable Than Ever

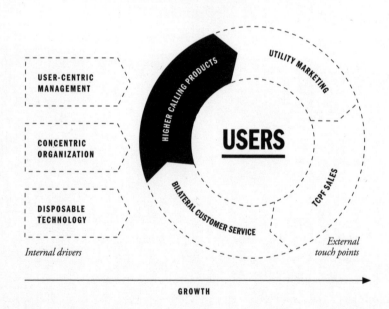

Twenty years ago, there were no users, only customers. The proliferation of digital media has ignited a revolution in the way consumers shop and in consumers' relationships with brands. Pre-Internet, let's say you wanted to go to San Diego for a long weekend of sunshine and golf. Your first stop was to your local travel agent who likely had a storefront office near your home or business. To service you, the agent would use her computer to access the Sabre network, a supplier of ticket and travel information not yet available to consumers. She would then present you with a couple of different itineraries and prices. You had no idea what else might be available, if ticket prices to San Diego were rising or falling, or how exactly you could adjust your travel dates and times for better prices. You could, if you wanted, call around to other agents, but that was time-consuming and inconvenient. Usually you just bought the best of what she offered. The same process would apply to choosing a hotel. The agent might have some brochure-type information about each option's various amenities, but it was almost impossible to know much about the actual environment, such as whether it was kid-friendly, noisy, or recently renovated. Usually the decisions came down to price and the brand you were most familiar with or loyal to. On the bright side, you could walk out of the travel agent's office with your trip fully booked.

A week or two before departure, you'd go to the mall. Your first stop would be the bookstore where you might find three guidebooks to San Diego largely indistinguishable outside of the name brand on the cover. You'd choose the brand you knew best and head to the counter to pay. Then the same thing happened at the luggage shop, where you ended up buying a Samsonite suitcase, and at The Gap, where you picked up a couple of pairs of khaki shorts.

Though you may not have given it any thought, all the buying decisions you made for your vacation were dependent on and limited by two things: proximity and brand. You went to businesses that were close because you had no access to businesses beyond your locale; because you had incomplete knowledge about a product, brand names became shorthand for quality; and because price shopping had to be done slowly with phone calls or physical trips to various stores, you usually were stuck accepting what "seemed" like a good price, rather than what you knew to be the best price.

Today everything has changed. Dependent customers have turned into empowered users. Your local travel agent has probably changed careers or retired. She was done in by Orbitz, Travelocity, Expedia, and the airlines' own Web sites. Now you could decide to spend hours fastidiously tracking how ticket prices would be affected by any possible alteration in itinerary. If you're wondering whether prices might rise or fall in the coming week, you can go to Bing to assess a chart of historical ticket prices and get the search engine's own recommendation of whether to buy or wait. Next you might dedicate hours to learning detailed information about hotels and car rental companies on consumer-review sites such as TripAdvisor and Yelp. And then you can research the dozens of guidebooks available through Amazon, where you can also read reviews for the right piece of luggage, find its absolute lowest price, buy it, and then move on to research the universe of khaki shorts.

The Internet has dramatically transformed the way we buy things. Consumer decisions are no longer limited by a lack of information and choice. Rather, users are in charge of their consumerism with boundless information about prices and products, and most of all with unrestrained choice. For businesses, the digital era has brought with it a flood of challenges:

- **The elimination of geographical barriers to competition.** Because businesses no longer need to be located in close physical proximity to their customers, they've been pummeled by an explosion of competition. Any company based anywhere from Delhi to Delaware with a UPS shipping account can sell nearly the same products as a local brick-and-mortar business to the same customers.

- **The democratization of the production of goods and services.** Anyone can become the competition. Think you have a revolutionary design for, say, khaki pants? You can go online to Alibaba.com, find a low-cost manufacturer, start selling them on eBay and Amazon, and boom—you're a competitor to every other khaki pants maker on the market.

- **The full transparency of pricing.** Multiple Web sites are dedicated to providing consumers with price comparisons including Kayak as well as Nextag, PriceGrabber, and TheFind. The proliferation of smart phones is only making it easier to evaluate prices. The Red Laser iPhone and Android app, for example, lets you go to a store, scan the bar code on a product, and instantly see what the product sells for in nearby stores and online.

  If your company doesn't offer the best price, there's no way to hide it—not from your shoppers or from your competitors. This means that in an attempt to avoid risking losing sales to savvy shoppers, retailers often chase each other's prices to the lowest possible point. In July 2010, executives from Soap.com, an online drugstore, watched as Amazon systemically pinged twenty-five thousand items on the site and then adjusted its prices to match.

- **Quality has become transparent.** The use of brands as proxies for quality has diminished as consumers can so readily access in-depth product information. Today, while you could still go to Best Buy and talk to its salespeople, as you might have done fifteen years ago, you can also read professional reviews at CNET, check out what other customers have to say on Amazon, and solicit trusted opinions from your Facebook network. Or, if you're not stuck between two products, but rather need help choosing the perfect television set, you can go to a site like Measy or Hunch that gives customized recommendations based on a user's answers to a series of questions. The easier it gets to use the Internet to compare product details across brands, the less compelling a brand name is in purchasing decisions. Forrester reports that about one-half of online men and 42 percent of female Internet users consult online product reviews and ratings at least once a month.

All of these innovations turn into one giant problem for businesses: widespread commoditization. It is increasingly rare for consumers to perceive branded items as unique in the marketplace; brand names no longer enjoy automatic premium pricing because there is no longer an assumption of superior quality; and virtually every product and service provider faces intense pricing pressure due to the transparency available online. Then as brands drop prices or lose sales, they have to cut costs internally, which further minimizes the difference between their premium branded product and the competitor's nameless one. It's a dangerous cycle, but there is a way out.

WINNING WITH VALUE

The winner doesn't have to be the one with the lowest price; it can also be the one that provides shoppers with the most vibrant and valuable experience—what I refer to as a company's higher calling. A higher calling is a company's mission to become more valuable to its customers than the physical products it sells—and not through empty marketing messaging. The company must provide a service that genuinely offers its customers improvements in their quality of life. That's exactly what Diapers .com did.

Diapers.com launched in 2005 with the ambition of owning the online market for selling baby products, starting with diapers. The goal sounded somewhat quixotic. The diapers market is already mature, highly commoditized, and dominated by heavyweights such as Walmart, Costco, Target, and Amazon. But it's also a sign of the times: a start-up believed it could jump into a well-established market and prevail.

The first months were indeed rocky. To compete in earnest, Diapers .com needed more than a Web site, it needed to be able to buy the product for wholesale prices. This meant convincing Procter & Gamble to welcome them into its stable of retailers. Not an easy feat. At first, P&G wouldn't budge, so a Diapers.com employee who lived on Long Island had to drive to local discount stores and buy up their supplies of diapers in order to fulfill the orders coming in. This process forced Diapers.com to take a loss on every sale, but it accepted this as a part of getting established. And that was a good bet. Eventually Procter & Gamble relented and began to deal directly with the start-up—a green light Diapers.com needed to move to the next stage of its plan.

"We needed to be more efficient than anyone else out there," says Diapers.com CEO Marc Lore. So he and his cofounder, Vinit Bharara, hired a nuclear physicist to help. The scientist was tasked with identifying opportunities to shave shipping costs. To do this he crunched data on typical customer orders, box sizes, and UPS shipping rates, then he wrote an algorithm that could determine the most efficient way to pack products for the cheapest shipping. As a result, Diapers.com stocks twenty-three different box sizes, and each one gets packed as tightly as possible. This precision saves the company about one dollar per shipment, or 1 percent of the average hundred-dollar order. Another proprietary algorithm calibrates the exact amount of inventory the company needs to have on hand at any given time. And where people would be too slow or costly, machines are doing the work. At the company's warehouse in Gouldsboro, Pennsylvania, 260 robots help to pick and move orders. "We live and die by the ability to get our products shipped out as fast and at low cost as possible," Lore says. This focus on efficiency means that Diapers.com doesn't only sell at low prices, it delivers to anywhere in the country within two days; orders from Manhattan generally arrive on the same day.

Diapers.com has seen great success. In 2010, the company announced it was expecting to deliver five hundred million diapers, about four times the number sold by Amazon, the closest online competitor. And then for the icing on the cake, in November, Amazon bought the whole company for $545 million. The trajectory from a garage in Long Island to a half-billion-dollar payday in five years is the type of overnight win only possible in today's democratized, digitally powered market.

Sound too good to be true? Here's the catch. Diapers.com competes closely on diaper prices. Any diaper shopper can go online, compare prices, notice the deals on Diapers.com, and decisively click to buy from them. But diapers only provide a gross profit margin of 9 percent. So how was Diapers.com surviving and thriving on the sale of such a commodity? How could it pay for such expedient shipping? How could it afford

260 robots and a nuclear physicist? It couldn't have. And it didn't. Only Walmart has the model to win on price and still pay the bills.

Diapers.com relies on strategies above and beyond winning on price. In fact, the low cost of diapers and the efficiency with which they're shipped to customers are just two tactical elements of the company's higher calling. The premise is simple: parents have busy, hectic lives and Diapers.com is there to help remove the stress and headache. Its diapers are cheap and immediately delivered so parents don't have to worry about having basic parental necessities on hand. This passion flows though the company: its Web site is incredibly user-friendly and offers a baby registry and tools for parents to easily reorder products; its return policy is simple and lenient; and its customer-service representatives are incredibly helpful and kind. Diapers.com isn't in the business of selling diapers; it's in the business of preventing parents' headaches and stress. Its customers know that Diapers.com will quickly and effectively take care of their product needs for their babies. "We've trained our employees to say, 'This is not just a business. We're there to help customers and make their day better,'" Lore says. "And that's really sparked a lot of viral word of mouth." It's also sparked sales of other items such as strollers, car seats, and toys, which bring in a much higher profit margin than the flagship product.

A HIGHER CALLING

Diapers.com wins because it solves a larger problem than the more mundane issues addressed by a case of diapers: it simplifies parents' lives. And that deeply user-centric point of view makes Diapers.com worth more to moms and dads than its competitors: it inspires them to use Diapers.com for the purchase of higher-margin items, and as a result it counteracts the powerful tide of commoditization. Here are a few other examples of companies with well-executed higher callings.

- **IKEA** sells affordable, pragmatic furniture. It's not alone in this market. There are many stores that do this too, including Target, Walmart, and Kmart. But IKEA is different. People decorate their whole homes with its products. People travel hours to get to the store, spend even more hours assembling the furniture, and then they go online to sites such as www. Ikeahackers.net to share the ingenious ways they've chosen to customize their products. Millions of people see IKEA as a place that offers easy access to a comfortable, stylish home. IKEA's higher calling is to help people have better everyday lives.

- **Netflix** is just a movie rental service, like Blockbuster, iTunes, and on-demand services from cable providers. But Netflix subscribers rely on the company to manage and supply their entire movie-watching agenda. To them, Netflix isn't just a generic library of movies to rent. It's their personal hub of video—people trust Netflix to provide an evening of entertainment. This is Netflix's higher calling.

- **Nutrisystem** sells a dieting program that consists of meals being delivered to members every month. But Nutrisystem doesn't see itself solely as a food delivery service and dieting program—and neither do its customers. It positions itself as a company teaching healthy living. One user in particular created her own Web site to share how Nutrisystem taught her how to stop overeating and lose forty-five pounds. And her site's become so popular, she opened a forum for all Nutrisystem users to share their experiences. Many commenters echo her sentiment about the company teaching them good eating habits and helping them feel fit. Nutrisystem's higher calling is to help people have a healthy, feel-good life.

- **Herman Miller**, leader in its industry in the Digital Leadership Set, sells office furniture. But Herman Miller fans don't see interchangeable, generic items—they see innovative, high-performance, eye-grabbing products such as the Aeron and Mirra chairs. This isn't by accident. After the dot-com bust of the early 2000s, the office furniture industry went into a deep tailspin. Herman Miller executives looked ahead and saw their margins shrinking further as Chinese competition increased. The only way to thrive, they decided, was to differentiate with truly great products. So they invested tens of millions of dollars into research and development. "We don't define ourselves as an office furniture company or even a furniture company," said CEO Brian Walker. "Our boundary is around people and human performance . . . problem-solving design is at the core of what Herman Miller is." The company is not just about giving workers a place to sit; its higher calling is to help people at work, school, and home perform better and more comfortably.

- **Chase** sells banking services: checking accounts, savings accounts, credit cards—pretty dry stuff. But in 2008, Chase distinctively positioned itself as a bank that serviced users not simply by having more ATMs or launching better reward programs, but by dedicating itself to keeping up with the rapid changes in consumer behavior. This strategy was launched with the tagline "Chase What Matters" after research showed, "as new technologies emerge, people's lifestyles and expectations change significantly." At the time, nearly seventy million people used online banking, but Chase only had 6.8 percent of the online banking market. It knew it had to catch up and stay relevant or fall behind. Its first step, defining its mission: to provide financial services that "keep(s) up with the needs and desires of people with busy, dynamic lifestyles." Chase wanted to be the bank that consistently fit most naturally, conveniently into users' daily lives . . . being more than just a checking account. Chase's true higher calling? Convenience.

BUILDING THE HIGHER CALLING

All of these companies use digital technologies, as well as offline amenities where applicable, to holistically create deeply user-focused experiences that complement their core products and services, fight the gravity of commoditization, and ultimately gain a competitive advantage in the market. Here's how:

- **IKEA** positions itself as a resource for a better everyday life by presenting shoppers with information, amenities, and tools that make shopping for furniture and crafting a well-designed room easier than it would be shopping anywhere else. As far as digital media goes, it uses its Web site not just as a venue for showcasing its products, but as a platform for user guidance. It provides lessons on getting the most out of your TV room, reviving a room's look without buying new furniture, and how to "furnish a room with light." It also provides a 3-D modeling tool for kitchens, so users can design their dream place to play chef. These elements are complemented offline with IKEA's innovative and practical furniture designs, in-store child care, and inexpensive, family friendly meals of Swedish meatballs for just $3.99. From shopping in-store or on the Web site to the everyday use of the products, Ikea presents users with the seamless experience of its higher calling.

- **Netflix** is not your typical movie rental service. It provides users with much more than just an online catalogue of movies for rent—as was described in chapter 3. It built a stellar personalized recommendation engine that helps subscribers choose just the right film to watch; it offers users a tool to build their own running queue of movies they want to see, which many people maintain with regularity; and it's fully relieved at-home movie watchers of the often lengthy quest to choose just the right movie by hunting through a video store's genre-based aisles and limited in-stock selection.

  Netflix is truly a user's hub for video entertainment. And this dedication to meeting user needs has allowed the company to nimbly shift its business model from DVD mail delivery to online streaming. The firm prioritizes providing entertainment to consumers in whatever format they want. This type of agility can only be grasped when the company is more dedicated to its users than its present business model—a dedication that differentiated it from its brick-and-mortar, legacy competitor, Blockbuster. The result: people trust Netflix to fully manage and optimize their movie-watching leisure time.

- **Nutrisystem** steps from its base role as provider of diet plans and food, and rises to meet its users' higher-order desire to be healthier by using its Web site to provide free, unlimited, 24/7 counseling, a community of fellow Nutrisystem users, and classes and articles about health and fitness. These resources guide its users toward their real goal, which isn't the purchase of more meals, but a healthy lifestyle—a far cry from the faddish diets and miracle weight-loss cures offered by the competition.

- **Herman Miller** doesn't just hawk places for people to sit. It endeavors to meet its users' higher-order desire for better performance and comfort at work, school, and home. The brand serves this calling by its aforementioned investment in research and development, and by offering users an information-rich Web site that includes research reports on subjects such as how to build a healthy work culture, how to help older workers be comfortable in the workplace, and how to give employees personal control over their lighting. There's a section on proper ergonomics, as well as case studies on how other companies and organizations have outfitted their offices. One section of the site features blog posts on the latest developments in areas such as design innovation. The company's Twitter stream also shares news in design and employee well-being. Taken as a whole, Herman Miller can help anyone learn how to build a pleasurable and productive environment.

- **Chase** stepped up to embody its higher calling of keeping pace with user behavior and naturally fitting into consumers' daily lives by taking the lead of the mobile banking market. Its iPhone app debuted in 2008 and by the end of 2010, it had been downloaded more than two million times. Android mobile phone users downloaded the app five hundred thousand times in just two weeks. With the free program, users can send money to a friend, get account status updates, pay bills, see transaction history—and make deposits. In July 2010, Chase introduced QuickDeposit, a system that lets its customers deposit checks by taking photos of them with their mobile phones. It supported this breakthrough in user-centric technology with a Super Bowl XLV commercial showcasing the service. Chase was also the first U.S. bank to produce an iPad app. These initiatives fit perfectly with user behavior, and Chase's higher calling. As of November 2010, 29 percent of Americans under forty used their phones for banking at least once a month and 36 percent reported no longer visiting banks. With this focus on mobile technology, Chase gave its customers what they wanted: one less reason to see a teller.

IKEA, Netflix, Nutrisystem, Herman Miller, and Chase have all identified user needs that are greater than those their products alone could satisfy and have innovated in ways to directly meet these needs. It is this central focus on users that differentiates them from their competition and fights the gravitational pull of commoditization.

Each company's solution may seem distinctive and unique to its particular business. But when you take a step back, you'll see that their strategies, and those of other companies that have activated their greater intentions, all use at least one of four common tactics:

1. They create a "decision service."

2. They develop services complementary to their core offering.

3. They combine their analog products with digital to create an entirely new offering.

4. They use data to differentiate.

DECISION SERVICES

By "decision service," I'm referring to anything that helps consumers make sense of the mass of choice and information of the online shopping process, helping them find just the right thing to buy. We've all gone down the rabbit hole researching products for hours and hours before buying, and not just for complex items such as electronics but random items such as candles, bug sprays, and area rugs. Curating the shopping experience to help the user complete his or her purchase without compromising choice satisfies a basic need that every online shopper has. As such, this is one of the most common ways businesses realize their higher callings. Usually this decision service comes in one of three forms:

- **The wealth-of-information approach.** If the company's Web site provides ample information about a product, the shopper will become favorably exposed to the firm's offerings. This develops a sense of trust in the company's authority, motivating consumers to loyally follow its advice and buy from them. The information provided often goes beyond product specifications from the manufacturer and includes detailed product comparisons and usage information. For example, HomeDepot.com offers thorough how-to articles and videos about almost any home improvement project, from installing hanging light fixtures to directions for safely leaning a ladder against the side of a house. This content positions Home Depot as the go-to source for DIY home improvement information, and within this content the user can find the products required to complete the DIY project, all of which are available for sale. This wealth-of-authoritative-information strategy holds true for all sorts of companies, not just mainstream retailers. IBM, for example, has extensive case studies and information to help companies select and use the right technology for their industry. Similarly, McKesson, the health care supply chain company, operates a Web site, HighPerformancePharmacy.com, that helps pharmacy managers run their business better—and implicitly, choose the right McKesson solutions.

- **Prefabricated shopping lists.** Amazon does it. So does Home Depot and myriad other retailers. When a user clicks on a product, these sites present them not only with the item of choice, but with complementary items that when used with the original item are more likely to solve a customer's overall, higher calling problem. Click on a bathroom vanity on Home Depot.com and get recommendations for matching mirrors. Click on a coffeemaker on Amazon and see suggestions for replacement water and coffee filters. Derivatives of this technique are user-generated lists such as wish lists, registries, and the more cutting-edge function, shopping history lists. This is what grocery delivery company Fresh Direct does. The first time you buy from Fresh Direct, you need to search through the site, find each item you want, and add it to your shopping cart. When you return for another purchase, the site posts a list of what you bought before. So if you want to buy it again, all you have to do is simply check a box indicating you'd like to put this item in your current cart, and enter the quantity you'd like. After a few visits, you have a checklist of all the grocery items you order on a regular basis, which makes shopping at the site incredibly efficient and eliminates the frustration of going to the grocery store only to get home and realize you forgot to get the milk.

- **Peer pressure.** User-generated content about products such as reviews or usage ideas is a particularly persuasive decision service. Consumers regularly consider user reviews to be more credible than official corporate information. They appear to be from an objective third party who has experience with the product, and often contain more nuanced information than whatever promotional copy the manufacturer or retailer wrote. I'm confident we've all experienced this in our own shopping proclivities, but just to prove it, in a recent ExpoTV study, 92 percent of moms reported trusting consumer reviews more than the manufacturer's description of products. Other forms of social interactions work as decision services too, and what's more, they lure the user to spend extended time engaging with the company. At Burberry's ArtoftheTrench.com, users submit photos of themselves or others wearing a Burberry trench coat. And then the community rates, comments on, and shares the photos. Participating in the program mimics the sensation of critiquing and being inspired by a strangers' personal style— but it's all about Burberry. This concept of peer informed decision making also comes to life on the extremely popular fashion site Polyvore. Polyvore allows fashion enthusiasts to create collages of apparel and accessories to share with each other and then shop from.

The challenge for brands is that peer pressure, also called social shopping (which we'll discuss more in chapter 6, "TCPF Sales") is becoming more and more common. Users are increasingly expecting user reviews to be part of all their purchasing activities. So the key to differentiation is to build a community and an experience that is unique to the brand, as Burberry has done, rather than relying on plain old user reviews.

COMPLEMENTARY SERVICES

The second common technique for activating a higher calling is to establish a complementary service that meets a user need not satisfied by competitor businesses. This tactic often comes to life through member-only articles, tools, and social experiences. Netflix does this with its program that allows subscribers to maintain a queue of movies to watch and get personalized movie recommendations. Nutrisystem does it with its online community of peers and counselors.

American Express, a Digital Leadership Set member, is also doing this through its OPEN Forum. On www.OpenForum.com, American Express offers small business owners, who are also card members, a multifaceted digital experience dedicated to valuable content, connections, and community, according to Jason Rudman, who runs it. Qualified users can go online to create a profile about themselves and their small business; send each other messages; read articles and watch videos on everything from managing employees to using social media for marketing; comment on this content; receive a list of member businesses they might be interested in buying services from; become included in this list that's sent to other members; show up in member search results; and gain access to conferences and trade shows. It's a treasure trove of small business networking opportunities and social engagement for like-minded individuals—and at one point more than two million unique monthly visitors used it. This level of activity demonstrates that American Express has pinpointed and executed its higher calling with great precision—small business owners are hungry to connect and discuss the issues facing their businesses with the intent of using this knowledge to become more successful. In pursuing this higher calling, AMEX hopes that when the site's users need financial products, they'll think of American Express.

An interesting challenge for companies is whether these complementary services are offered to any user, or whether they're only available to members. If free, they're also marketing vehicles, serving as a gateway for users to become customers; if only available to paying customers, complementary services become strong customer retention vehicles. In the above examples, Nutrisystem and American Express both provide ample free services to attract the not-yet-paying users; Netflix's recommendation engine is only an option for subscribers.

The best digital organizations structure complementary services as a hybrid of free and paid, so they realize a service's potential to be both a lead generation and a customer-retention vehicle. Ideally, the free version exposes to the user the benefit of being a paying customer. For example, Nutrisystem's community is free to everyone—and as a result it's a great source of paying customers. The people on the dieting program who use the site help spread the message to the nonsubscribers they interact with that truly effective dieting only becomes possible with the Nutrisystem food subscription. And, if you are a customer, more services become available—for example, getting connected to a mentor. In the process, the free complementary service gracefully becomes a more powerful service when the user starts paying.

CREATING A WHOLLY NEW OFFERING

The most sophisticated companies take the idea of a complementary service to an extreme by truly combining the analog and digital world to create an entirely new offering, one that is not possible without combining the physical and virtual world. The result is a single new solution that's more valuable than any pure offline or online product. Nike Plus is an excellent example of this.

At its most basic, Nike Plus is a system that helps users keep track of their workout statistics. To get started, you place an inexpensive Nike brand sensor in your athletic shoe—which doesn't have to be made by Nike. This sensor then relays data to your iPod as you work out. For runners, a voice in your headphones then keeps you alerted to your speed, distance covered, and calories burned. When you hook up your iPod to your computer, the data gets relayed to the Nike Plus Web site. From there, you can examine your own results and also compare them with thousands of others around the world. You can also interact with other runners in novel ways. For example, if you set a goal to run a hundred miles a month, you can go online and either form your own group with that goal or find an existing one—a likely scenario, since there are more than three million members. It's a piece of gear still at the cutting edge of fitness equipment five years after its introduction.

Nike Plus realizes the shoemaker's higher calling of helping people achieve their full athletic potential. As one aspiring athlete and Nike consumer, SeeFluffy, said at the opening of a ten-minute YouTube video (viewed more than two thousand times) about Nike Plus: "You can't buy your way to fitness. Just because you go buy this item, it doesn't mean that you're automatically going to knock two minutes off your time or that you're going to lose ten pounds, it just means you have another tool to use to help you and encourage you on your journey."

Although it's not necessary to buy Nike shoes to participate, it seems that many have: Nike executives credit the program with boosting the company's share of the running shoe market from 48 percent in 2006 to 61 percent in 2008. "We see the relative market share that we gain from other brands and it gives us a tremendous opportunity," says Stefan

Olander, Nike's vice president of digital sport. "If someone is used to running in another brand and they like another brand, once you start using Nike Plus you have a really good reason to try out Nike's line of shoes."

Nike is so advanced in its digital integration that it actually uses this technique to address a wholly different higher calling. For sneaker buyers who want their shoes to directly represent their own unique fashion sense, Nike offers NikeID: a Web-based program that allows shoppers to design their own pair of Nikes. Users pick a blank shoe canvas and then the color of every element from laces to the Nike swoosh logo. They can even have a word like their nickname printed on a tab on the heel. To users of this service, Nike is more than a manufacturer of athletic shoes; the company is acknowledging its consumers' individuality and empowering them to express it.

Another company that has excelled at combining offline products with digital technologies is Ford, a top performer in the Digital Leadership Set. Through its Ford SYNC initiative, Ford, in the words of *Fast Company*, is transforming the car into "the ultimate mobile device."

Here's how it works. If you own a Ford equipped with SYNC, your mobile phone will automatically connect to the system through Bluetooth technology. When you receive a call, the caller ID will appear on your dashboard. To answer the phone, you press a button on the steering wheel or give a voice command. Your call will be routed through the car's speakers—any music playing will automatically pause—and your voice is picked up through a microphone in the car. If you plug your iPod into the car, you can also control it through the steering wheel, or you can give it voice commands—the system recognizes ten thousand instructions—such as "Play jazz" or "Play Rolling Stones." Apps such as "Pandora" work in the car the same way.

New Fords also include an option for an eight-inch touch screen, called MyFord Touch. With this, people can insert SD cards to view pictures, plug in a video camera (only when the car is in park), or browse through the music on their MP3 players with the touch screen. As of May 2011, this technology will be updated to offer Ford buyers a roving, car-based Wi-Fi hot spot. In essence, Ford has melded driver's digital lives with the experience of driving a car.

This initiative has helped Ford thrive while Chrysler and General Motors, the other members of the Big Three, have had a more difficult time competing in today's recessionary environment. Ford reported that in SYNC's first year, one-third of Ford buyers were sold by the option. By 2011, more than three million SYNC units, which cost $395 each, had been installed in Ford cars; 80 percent of Ford buyers opted to include the unit. But perhaps the greatest measure of SYNC's success was that in 2011 General Motors announced it was launching a "me-too" product, the Chevrolet MyLink. It'll be hard for them to catch up, though. Ford has already gone a long way toward redefining its higher calling from selling cars that will get you around town with a minimum of flash, to becoming a company that keeps people plugged in while they're on the move. "We saw people becoming addicted to connectivity," said Derrick Kuzak, Ford's product development chief, "and we connected the dots." For any car company to usurp Ford's user-first position it would have to make revolutionary strides in usability—a highly unlikely proposition in the near future. The SYNC is just that great.

DATA DIFFERENTIATION

A final technique companies use to activate their higher calling is data collection, analysis, and use. When users sign up with Web sites or other digital products, the brands behind them track their activities. The companies can then pool this data in clever ways that make their higher calling services even more valuable to users. This approach also allows companies to take advantage of the network effect: the value of the service improves with each additional user, making it even harder for a new service to emerge that can be of similar quality. And, it creates lock-in— the more data a user has in the system, the more costly it is to switch and enter his data elsewhere.

Nike Plus is also an excellent illustration of data differentiation. For every runner who signs up for Nike Plus, the site collects more and more data about runners and their training routines. Nike then takes the data, crunches it, presents it, and ultimately adds an enormous amount of value to it. For example, anyone using the program can compare his training routines and times to other runners around the world. This also creates lock-in; once someone has entered five runs into the Nike Plus system, she is likely to stick with it. Since Nike's software already contains the results of all a person's past runs, there is a big disincentive for a user to switch to a competitor. Because of its expert use of data, Nike builds additional brand affinity every time someone uses the software.

Netflix's recommendation engine is similarly dependent on customer data. It tracks subscriber movie choices and ratings, and then provides personalized recommendations based on this activity. For example, if someone rented *No Country for Old Men* and *Pulp Fiction*, Netflix might suggest *Trainspotting*. Or because someone watched *District 9* and *Stranger Than Fiction*, Netflix may suggest *Wall-E*. Every time a subscriber adds a movie to his queue or rates one, he gets more personalized movie ideas. The result is that Netflix helps customers discover films they'll enjoy and avoid ones they'll dislike—with recommendations that can be better than those provided by a friend.

The recommendation engine is so important to Netflix that in 2006 CEO Reed Hastings launched a competition to see if anyone could improve on the accuracy of Netflix's proprietary system by at least 10 percent. Lured by a million-dollar prize, thousands of teams from more than a hundred countries entered. Contestants accessed a fraction of anonymized Netflix data and started analyzing more than a hundred million customer movie recommendations. In September 2009, an international team of statisticians, machine-learning experts, and computer engineers won the prize by achieving a 10.06 percent improvement over Netflix's original predictive capabilities.

Hastings called this program a bargain for Netflix; in the end, every great prediction made by the company's recommendation engine decreases the likelihood that the user will use a service like iTunes, or just forget about movies altogether and turn on a football game. "It's doubling the quality of our movie recommendations and that helps our subscribers get more enjoyment from movies, because more often they love the movie they watch," Hastings says. "If every movie is incredible, you start to watch more."

DISCOVERING AND DEVELOPING A HIGHER CALLING

If a company isn't built from the ground up to answer a higher calling, becoming a higher calling–driven company can be quite disruptive. Of course the final outcome is a better, stronger company. But the path to really harnessing this advantage often requires businesses to make adjustments at the core of their existing business models. Here are two stories of vastly different organizations that made the change: Nutrisystem and the American Society of Mechanical Engineers.

Nutrisystem began redefining its online presence in 2007, at a time when the Pennsylvania-based company was just emerging from a checkered history. Founded in 1972, it was originally a franchise operation of diet centers that sold liquid protein shakes. As that fad fell out of favor in the late 1970s, the company retooled and began to sell prepackaged meals meant to limit calorie intake. Through the 1980s, Nutrisystem grew until it rivaled Weight Watchers as the world's largest weight loss company. In the early 1990s, though, it was hit with a wave of customer lawsuits that claimed its food caused gallstones. Nutrisystem won the legal battles, but the company lost sales and went bankrupt in 1993. A billionaire subsequently bought it and added clinics where doctors prescribed Fen-Phen diet drugs, a practice that ended when Fen-Phen was found to cause fatal heart problems. Then in 1999, the company jumped wholeheartedly on the dot-com bandwagon. It closed its retail locations, moved to an Internet sales model, renamed itself Nutrisystem.com, and went public. Its stock price briefly soared until the crash brought it plummeting to earth.

The company's turnaround began at the turn of the millennium when a new ownership group bought it. The new CEO revamped its food offerings to be based around a diet of low-glycemic index foods and meals designed for program adherents to lose two pounds a week. A month's supply of packaged food, which is meant to be supplemented by fresh fruits and vegetables, costs around three hundred dollars. To sell the meal plans, the company launched an aggressive direct response model, hawking its food through TV infomercials and magazine advertisements that featured "before and after" photos of successful customers. This tactic was tremendously effective: between 2002 and 2007, revenues climbed from $28 million to nearly $800 million. The company finally seemed to be heading in the right direction.

Except for one thing—the performance of the Web site was lacking. So Nutrisystem hired Chris Terrill, an executive who had formerly held positions at Match.com and Blockbuster.com, to lead Nutrisystem's e-commerce business. His first task during his tenure: revamp Nutrisystem. com with a goal of pushing sales and more deeply engaging consumers in the program.

At the start, Nutrisystem's Web site appeared to be an extension of the company's direct response business model. It was more like a digitized pamphlet than anything immersive or able to generate an emotional experience from visitors. Terrill wanted users to get the information they needed to really understand the product, but he also wanted them to feel good about buying it. He wanted users to "feel this was something that was substantive, that was meaningful, that it could help them transform their lives," he says. This would become Nutrisystem's higher calling—if only it could activate it.

Terrill began by deciding the company needed to offer much more information about its products online, including in-depth stories from people who had been on the program. He then expanded this idea about product information to apply to information about dieting, fitness, and a healthy lifestyle. One way this insight came to life is the "Mindset Makeover," a thirteen-week interactive program that helps users reorient their attitudes toward food and eating through videos, expert advice, tutorials, and tips. The company also developed online diet logs so members could enter and track their personal data, guides for dining out, a Web-based food diary, and exercise plans. Users can also get free online counseling or participate on message boards where other dieters share advice and provide mutual support.

Suddenly Nutrisystem.com was about community, self-expression, and healthy living. "If the 'before' Nutrisystem.com was something that was out of shape, sluggish, didn't make sense and was having a hard time doing some of the basic things that it wanted to do, the 'after' was svelte and smart and engaging and a completely different experience," Terrill says.

The redesign showed immediate results. First there was a rise in the number of people who bought the product after visiting the site. Then over time, the company has found that users active in the Nutrisystem .com community stay with the program longer than those who are not. It makes people feel engaged in the program; then the longer they stay, the more weight they lose, and the closer they get to reaching their goals. In the process, Nutrisystem went from being just another diet that people try to a company that helps people achieve the weight, body, and lifestyle they desire.

This online renovation was so compelling and powerful, Terrill says, it ended up being "the impetus that really began to push the entire organization to see that there was a different way of doing things." Four years after the original 2007 Web site redesign, the company's traditional media now completely follows its Web site. The Web site's brand imagery, its tone, and how it aims to motivate people, are all visible in the brand's offline products. For the company, Terrill says, it was a "total transformation."

The American Society of Mechanical Engineers went through a similar transition to Nutrisystem, only it knew its higher calling in advance and just wasn't delivering. ASME, which has been around since 1880, is one of the most important organizations you may have never heard of. One of its main functions is to establish uniform engineering codes and standards. For example, before such standards were set, fire departments in neighboring municipalities could be using different types of firefighting equipment. Those in one town might use square connectors to hook up their hoses to fire hydrants, while those in the next had round connectors. That meant if a fire crew was called to the next town, they might have to sit and watch a building burn down because they couldn't connect to the water supply. To address problems like that, ASME drew together committees of engineers to come up with industry standards for manufacturers. Right now, ASME distributes six hundred codes and standards used around the world for the design, manufacturing and installation of mechanical devices ranging from boilers to escalators to the cranes used in nuclear facilities. In addition, ASME, which has a membership of 120,000, has a stated higher calling: to advance the engineering profession, create bridges among different engineering fields, and promote the role of engineers in society.

ASME's Web site, however, did not match its higher-order mission statement. It was simply a place for engineers and companies to buy codes and standards when needed. And that was what drove most of its traffic. There was little content to engage users, be they engineers or members of the general public with an interest in the field.

When the organization began to think about a Web site redesign, its early research uncovered some sobering data about how badly their site needed to step up its game. ASME discovered there were more than 300,000 mechanical engineers on LinkedIn versus its 120,000 own community members. Amazon sold 1,600 mechanical engineering books for its Kindle; ASME sold just 77 e-books. An online job board listed 34,000 mechanical engineering jobs, while ASME listed just 618. "We saw that engineers are trying to connect with other engineers outside of ASME," says Nakiso Maodza, the digital project manager at ASME overseeing the redesign. "We decided to try and change that."

Its first step was to survey the membership to see what they wanted from the site. ASME then used this information to define four different user personas and needs the site could satisfy. These included:

- The practicing engineer who was a project manager or company executive. She would be interested in using ASME.org to keep abreast of important trends in the field.

- The working engineer who was more of a specialist or an academic. He would want information targeted specifically to the niche in which he worked.

- The student who was looking for career guidance to excel in the field. She would want information on how to bridge the transition from academic to professional life.

- The support worker who went to the site to buy codes and standards. He would want easy access to the products he visited the site to buy.

This last one was ASME's only existing user. The rest would be new. And the question was how to get the others involved. It chose to take a largely "complementary services" approach. It would attract its full breadth of members to the site and add value to ASME membership by making the destination a source of highly relevant and engaging content for all personas.

To achieve this goal, the site's strategy for choosing and presenting the content would be integral to success. One tactic the team explored has been to put lighthearted content upfront as an entry point for professionals, students, and engineering enthusiasts alike. These articles would then be linked to other areas of the site with more complex information. The user can follow the links to the extent of his interest, all the while being exposed to headlines about the field at large and the significant role mechanical engineering plays in the world. "We want to tie things together—current news, developments in engineering, conferences we are having, books we are selling—so that people can see everything that's going on across the field," Maodza says.

Say an expert in tribology—which focuses on the friction between objects as they interact with each other in motion—went to the site for information relevant to his niche. On his way to his target content, he may come upon a story profiling a recent mechanical engineering graduate who consults for a television show that speculates about what type of historical fighters would win in battle such as a Spartan versus a Ninja. Or he could read a story featuring a compelling headline such as "Four More Bolts Would Have Done It, They Would Have Saved Us," about the Deepwater Horizon oil spill in the Gulf of Mexico. "We're really pushing the organization to say, 'A big engineering disaster happened, and here's an analysis,'" Maodza says. "We want this to be a place where engineers can come, get information, and then have analysis and a case study to find out why these things happened. And students can come and find out about what they can do in the field, and why it's important."

All of the content would ultimately facilitate an online conversation about matters of interest to all members of the field and attract them to further engage with ASME. And this would undoubtedly support the organization's higher calling.

The new product vision is scheduled to be released in phases over time; the first was launched in March 2011. But before the initial launch, and even though the organization's higher calling was long defined, Maodza says the new direction of the site has functioned to change the organization's perceived role in its community. "To me, this is where digital becomes powerful," Maodza says. "The evolution of the Web site forces the organization to rethink how it serves its audience and constituents. It's about how ASME makes its industry more compelling." Maybe its higher calling is going to grow even greater.

Every company discussed in this chapter is selling a service or a product that solves a basic user need. Diapers, home and office furniture, athletic shoes, movie rentals, prepared meals for weight loss, home improvement supplies, credit cards, trench coats, membership in a trade association—they all satisfy a finite user need. But the customers buying these products have needs greater than buying a chair or signing up for a credit card; they need a comfortable place to work and a tool to help their small businesses grow. Companies can affordably begin to help users address this larger need by using digital technologies to create new and complementary services and products. This is the role that a brand used to play before the advent of the Internet—convincing customers that a soft drink isn't sugar water, it's happiness. But today empty brand promises are not enough. User-first brands must come to life in ways that exhibit their company values and demonstrate their prioritization of users—and this goes for marketing as well, which we discuss next.

CHAPTER SUMMARY: HIGHER-CALLING PRODUCTS

Market Insights

- Technology is commoditizing virtually all products and services. This is due to the elimination of geographical barriers to competition; the democratization of production; price transparency; and consumers' improved ability to assess quality through things like online product reviews.

- People are buying products to solve problems. Companies often incorrectly assume they're in the product development business as opposed to the business of solving a certain kind of problem for its customers. The problem a company is solving is called the "higher calling"—it's the bigger meaning behind the mundane product or service a business provides.

Strategic Imperatives

- Companies can embrace their higher calling to resist commoditization. This is possible by combing their "analog" product and service with a digital offering, all aligned with meeting their customer's problem. In doing so, companies can create a unique solution that's more useful to customers than the original standalone offering.

- The creation of a decision service—a service that helps people find the right product and use it properly—is a common way for companies to realize their higher callings. For example, a company can provide detailed information to help its customers select the right product; it can provide access to a wealth of information created by existing users to provide unfettered product data; and alternatively it can offer prebuilt lists of products that combine to solve a problem.

- Companies can also create services that are complementary to the core offering—namely, an online service that when used also helps the user solve his or her problems. For example,

Nutrisystem's food delivery service is an effective weight loss solution, but when combined with the use of Nutrisystem's online tools and community, it's more effective.

- Finally, companies can create a new product that spans analog and digital and is consistent with its higher calling. Netflix's expansion from mailing DVDs to streaming is a good example of this, as is Nike's development of its Nike Plus online training program that includes a physical device that attaches to your sneaker.

- Digital/analog higher calling solutions are most effective when they rely on proprietary company data, ideally data that grows and becomes more valuable as more people use the service. In doing so, organizations can utilize network effects to continually fight the trend toward commoditization.

5

Utility Marketing

Attract and Engage Users by Giving, Not Taking

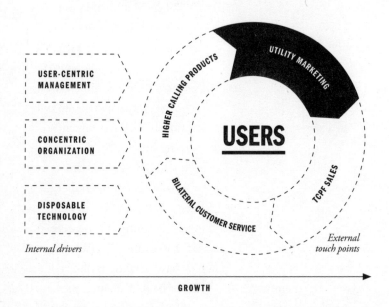

In 1994, AT&T was optimistic. It posted one of the first-ever banner ads on HotWired.com, a digital sibling to *Wired* magazine. The banner read, "Have you ever clicked your mouse right HERE? . . . You will!" At the time, clicking on a banner ad was a novelty; banner clicking was the future, they thought! AT&T was right that the future of the Internet would be marketing, but wrong about banners. Banners may be everywhere, but consumers have learned not to click.

The days of 468-x-60* banners were certainly simpler times. In the mid-'90s, when the Internet began to spread into the mainstream, advertisers thought all they had to do was put a flashy banner ad at the top of a Web page and users would eagerly click through to learn more. The strategy was a page from the mass-marketer's trusty playbook: blast a message to a captive audience that communicates the value of the brand via attention-getting story line or insightful tag line. This is how the great brands of our society were all built. It's how Coca-Cola taught the world to sing and Nike motivated athletes to "Just do it." There was no reason to think this approach wouldn't also work in digital.

At first this worked to a degree. Early on, when Internet users saw a banner ad, five out of every one hundred people who saw it clicked it (this is called a 5 percent click-through rate). When McDonald's put one of its 30-second TV commercials on America Online, in less than one month, 150 people dedicated 240 minutes to download the two-megabyte file. That might not sound like a lot of people, but considering how few users were online and how much time they spent getting a commercial message that had already been broadcast on TV for free, it's actually quite stunning.

But there were signs even then that the online environment was drastically different from traditional marketing outlets. In the same year as the AT&T and McDonald's ads, a Phoenix lawyer blasted out an ad about a green card lottery to news groups (early online bulletin boards used by the first adopters of the Internet). Within a few days of its existence, he received thirty thousand replies—both from prospective clients and users angry about the commercial intrusion. *The New York Times* covered the reaction to the ad: "He may have reached millions of people. But thousands of them were outraged that he had violated the unwritten rules of the electronic global community by sending unsolicited com-

---

* 468-x-60 refers to the width and height, in pixels, of banners that appear on Web pages. Once this was the standard size used on virtually all Web sites; today, while this size is still in use, it has been eclipsed by much larger banners, made possible by today's larger computer screens.

mercial messages." Core Internet users were rejecting the notion that they would allow themselves to be bombarded by brand messaging. They had higher expectations of usability on the Internet than the Phoenix lawyer had ever imagined.

Today, the mentality against intrusive advertising has won out. It's not just a limited community of early adopters concerned with tightly controlling their own online experiences and protecting usability—it's the whole ecosystem. In terms of marketing this means that a growing majority of users now ignore and reject almost all unwelcome brand messaging. Click-through rates on banner ads now average at less than one-half of 1 percent. This means less than one person in every two hundred people who see an ad clicks on it. Even worse, these infrequent clicks come from a small subsection of the Internet users. Each month only 16 percent of U.S. Internet users click on a display ad and most of the clicks come from an even smaller 8 percent of users, says market research firm comScore.

The rest of the Internet-using population barely even notices the banner ads at all—meaning these consumers are not receiving brand impressions. In a study done at HUGE, the research team monitored sixty people doing their normal online browsing for forty-five minutes. They checked the weather, looked for movie times, and watched YouTube videos. In that window, they were exposed to about twelve hundred banner ads. After they closed their browsers, we immediately asked them about the ads they had just seen. Strikingly, they couldn't even remember the ads from the last page they were on. All together, they recalled only about 2 percent of the display ads that they were shown. Even ads on the top of Web pages—generally the most expensive and considered the most effective—were easily ignored by users who quickly scrolled down the page to find the information they were looking for, often before the banner ad had even loaded.

Usability expert Jakob Nielsen has explained this phenomenon by doing experiments with computers decked out with sensors that track user eyeballs and capture what people look at on Web sites. He's found users don't look at ads; they even ignore page elements that appear adlike. If a user does catch a glimpse of an ad, which is rare, he might just glance at a corner in reaction to movement from animation or video. Or he might take in a design characteristic or two, but ignore the brand name and logo of the advertiser. Users are literally banner blind.

In many ways, the failure of display advertising is a culmination of a fifty-year trend: the decline of captive messaging. In the mythical fifties, consumers had limited media consumption choices—primarily the daily newspaper and three network television channels—and so the ability to reach a captive audience by marketers was high. Over time, technology enabled media proliferation, and the result was a decline in an advertiser's ability to reach a captive audience—the remote control, for example, as well as TiVo, were both great inventions that gave the consumers more choice and an increased ability to avoid advertiser messaging. The Internet represents the extreme: full consumer control, billions of media outlets, and little if any way to force consumers to pay attention to anything.

So what's a marketer to do? A glimpse at today's most successful brands tells the whole story. In 1995, when less than 20 percent of U.S. computer users had Internet access and Internet advertising was still novel, the nation's "best brands" were General Electric, Ford, and Sony, according to The Harris Poll. These are all brands that heavily use captive messaging like TV commercials. Fifteen years later, these powerful brands are still the same, still going strong, telling their story to the world. But there's a new addition to the top tier: Google. However, Google has barely spent a dollar on advertising. Instead, it became a massively successful brand with a completely user-first approach: it created a digital product that was highly useful to people, and because it was so practical and enjoyable, people spread the word about its value. Their simple formula—create a digital product that meets user needs—was enough to match the billions of dollars in marketing spent by the likes of Nike and Coca-Cola.

This emphasis on utility and users holds the key to effective marketing in the digital age. Several years ago, Jeff Bezos, founder, president, and CEO of Amazon, famously quipped, "Advertising is the price you pay for having an inferior product or service." While Amazon has since succumbed to advertising the Kindle on TV, his point remains the same: in the era of consumer control, people have to *want* to interact with your company and brand. People go online to solve problems, and consumers connect with the brands that meet user needs in a completely satisfying way. You can't just tell people you are great; you have to show it.

DO VERSUS TELL

In 2009 Pepsi had a problem. Sales of all soda brands had been down since 2005. To make matters worse, while there's much talk about people who are die-hard Pepsi lovers and people who will never drink anything but Coke, price what was most often driving sales. Whatever was on sale was what consumers purchased. Facing this reality, Pepsi was energized to make a change. So it threw out its well-worn marketing tactics and delved headfirst into user-centric marketing.

Pepsi knew:

- Some 86 percent of millennials reported they would buy from a charitable company versus one that's not.

- Almost nine out of ten people from ages eighteen to twenty-four would switch brands if another brand was associated with a good cause.

- Three out of four female baby boomers said they would choose a charitable company over one that is not.

- Sixty-six percent of the members of this group said they base their buying decisions on company business practices.

With this information in hand, supported by Pepsi's foundational belief in "Performance with Purpose" (a dedication to producing not just food that tastes good, but products that support local industry, the environment, and people's health), Pepsi's management decided that it would do something major to continue to push its brand toward its core values. The company wouldn't just run advertisements that would talk about "refreshing the world"; Pepsi would bring to life its brand meaning. Actions speak louder than words.

In December, as a lead-up to the February 2010 Super Bowl, Pepsi announced that for the first time in twenty-three years, it would not run any ads during the game. For a company that had spent $142 million on Super Bowl ads in the previous decade, this was huge news. Even more surprising was what Pepsi said it was going to do with the $20 million it would save by abstaining from the big game: It would put $20 million toward the Pepsi Refresh Project, an initiative with the goal of "refreshing" communities across the United States.

From a distance, the project appeared to be a large corporate philanthropy program. It was to be a year-long effort that encouraged individuals and organizations to apply for grants ranging from $5,000 to $250,000 in one of six categories: health, arts and culture, food and shelter, the planet, neighborhoods, and education. The project would accept up to a thousand submissions a month through RefreshEverything .com, and consumers would vote for the winning projects. Each month, Pepsi would contribute $1.3 million to support the fruition of ideas that refreshed communities across the nation. Up close it was a genius marketing move; the voting mechanism made the program social and became the engine for mass awareness.

Within a few weeks of the Web site's launch, before the first ideas were submitted and voting began, Pepsi became the subject of so much online chatter that even with its decision to forego Super Bowl advertising, Pepsi was one of the two most talked-about advertisers in the lead-up to the game. (The other was the conservative group Focus on the Family, which had filmed antiabortion ads starring quarterback Tim Tebow). The campaign received upward of five hundred million unpaid media impressions, and it engaged millions of visitors on its Web site and Facebook page.

Then right around the time the voting was due to begin, February 1, Pepsi launched a media blitz to support the project. The company advertised in outlets such as *People* magazine and the *Today* show, and used its public relations team to gain more media attention. For a time, the Pepsi Refresh Campaign was literally everywhere. Pepsi rang the bell at the New York Stock Exchange; it promoted the campaign at South by Southwest; celebrities took part to spur ideas and increase awareness; and marketing materials were present at grocery stores and other locations where Pepsi products were sold.

The campaign was also designed so that people would want to share it. For example, if you put up an idea that was in competition, you would naturally build a marketing campaign around it—you'd tweet about it, promote it on your Facebook page, and send out e-mail blasts to your network. You needed your whole network to vote on it to become a winner. Then when projects became finalists or winners, it was natural that local media such as television and newspapers ran stories on them. In effect, it was a giant grassroots campaign in which a thousand new contestants every month did everything they could to promote their ideas to help win the grants and to get votes. Of course, in doing so, they also promoted Pepsi.

When the competition officially opened, awareness of the project was so high it took just six days for a thousand proposed projects to fill the first month's quota. Among those first entries were:

- A request for $50,000 to build a community playground at an elementary school in Washington state.

- A proposal asking for $5,000 to help senior citizens care for their pets in Iowa.

- A $250,000 request from Teach for America to recruit and train teachers for low-income communities across America.

Month by month, the time it took for the monthly slots to fill up became shorter and shorter. By June 1, 2010, there were 80,000 ideas waiting in the Web site's queue for the 1,000 monthly openings. To get one of the sought-after slots, the 80,000 people behind these ideas needed to click to enter at exactly the right moment, similar to buying tickets for a high-demand live event. The June allotment filled up in just two minutes. By August it was thirty-two seconds.

Pepsi later extended the campaign with various offshoots. The first was a partnership with Major League Baseball in which each team in the league nominated one local project for a $200,000 grant. After the July

2010 Gulf of Mexico oil spill disaster, Pepsi announced that it was putting $1.3 million toward a special "Do Good for the Gulf" initiative. It would operate in the same way as the general Refresh Project, but for the improvement of communities directly affected by the disaster.

The campaign has been hugely successful. By September 2010, 42 million people had voted on the Pepsi Refresh Web site. By May 2011, over 80 million votes were accumulated on Pepsi Refresh—more votes than any presidential campaign in history. In one recent *Forbes* magazine study of major brands, Pepsi had climbed from the sixteenth most respected brand to fifth, the first time it ever beat Coke in that kind of survey. In 2011, the Pepsi Refresh Project expanded internationally, developing locally relevant executions of the program, while continuing to fund projects in the United States and Canada.

By creating something that has real utility and value for people, Pepsi, today the top performer in its industry in the Digital Leadership Set index, has drawn millions of consumers to its branded site. Users come because they are excited about the project, and research has shown that their perceptions of the brand change as they engage. And because the program is ongoing, this relationship with consumers is continuous— something that's not possible with television ads that come and go in thirty seconds.

Pepsi's approach is based on the notion of marketing in the name of helping users accomplish existing tasks, and literally prioritizing user experience over satisfying the compulsion to push a brand's own overtly sales-hungry messaging. Done correctly, this new way of marketing— what I call utility marketing—hands companies a prize greater than any hasty, inexpensive banner ad or spammy e-mail campaign could. It provides the company with user engagement. Users aren't just in a position to see (and ignore) a marketing message, they are interacting with the brand, appreciating the convenience or advantage the brand has provided, are likely sharing it with their social networks—and are being exposed to the marketing message all the while.

Utility marketing is at its core the merger of products and advertising. Advertising is all about telling people something. You have a message; you tell a story to communicate it; and you create desire for a product. Products, on the other hand, are the exact opposite. They're useful. You do something with them. Utility marketing creates desire by being useful.

This technique is effective because it's consistent with how people use the Web. As I said before, users aren't passive. They have unlimited choice and every click of the mouse is a user exercising that choice. Marketers therefore must create mechanisms for users to choose to be exposed to their marketing messages. And that happens when marketers create "brand utilities," products and services people choose to use, because they help them accomplish their tasks.

USERS ONLY GO WHERE THEIR NEEDS WILL BE MET

The best way to think about utility marketing is to approach it from the perspective of why users go online. User research at HUGE shows that people go online for two different reasons, reflecting two different sets of behaviors:

1. "I want to find or do something."

2. "Tell me what's new."

Let's start with the first one, "I want to find or do something." The browser is open and the user is trying to accomplish a specific goal: learn the scores for the latest games in the NCAA tournament, watch the TV show she accidentally deleted from her DVR, find out the weather, pay his bills, buy a new pair of rain boots, find a hint for a tough level on Angry Birds—the list could go on forever. The point is, users go online with a clear vision of the information they're looking for or the task they want to accomplish. So they open up the browser and go to one of two places, either directly to their destination (they knew the address or had bookmarked their go-to site) or to a "filter," a search engine such as Google or other online tools that help users find their destination. Every search engine and Web site has multiple links in it, such as advertisements or references to other articles, and those that appear relevant to the user's current task may very well be the next place he or she clicks.

Now for the second reason people go online, "Tell me what's new." Since the dawn of the Web, users have visited their e-mail inboxes to see what's new—all the latest messages that people have sent them. Facebook, instant messages, mobile texts, and Twitter are no different. They're just mailboxes decked out with a different interface and a different set of rules governing who receives what message. But one quality is consistent: messages in user mailboxes come from entities that the user has chosen to hear from. It's the checked box to receive company news at e-commerce checkouts, it's "liking" a brand on Facebook, it's following a brand on Twitter. And, for good reason, brands can struggle to penetrate this wall, because users have to agree to receive messages from a brand, and this is only possible if they think they're getting a lot of utility and value from the brand's messages. But when it works well, the user may forward it to a friend and this is a brand's first-class ticket into another user's mailbox. Because with it comes the endorsement of the sender.

These two user behaviors—"I want to do or find something" and "Tell me what's new"—form the basis of nearly all Web traffic. And both activities are fully grounded in the notion of the Internet as a platform for utility. People go online to accomplish a specific task, and they determine where to click by deciding if it's going to get them closer to their goal.

Putting this all together, Web traffic flows through what I call the "unified traffic framework." See Figure 8 on next page.

To go through this step by step, if the user wants to do or find something, he can go directly to a destination or have a filter, like a search engine, refer him to the right location. From this destination, the user can click around to other relevant pages or request messaging from the destination into his inboxes. If, on the other hand, the user wants to know what's new, he goes to his inbox (be it e-mail, Facebook, or Twitter) where he sees brand messages that lead him to a brand's destination.

The most effective marketing is integrated within all elements of this

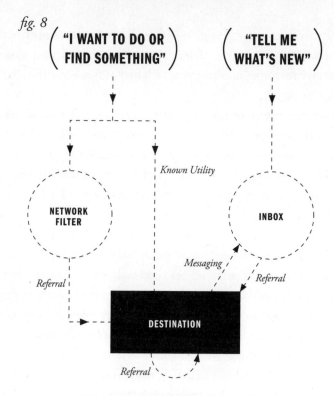

fig. 8

8. *The Unified Traffic Framework*

utility-driven traffic framework (it's a destination, it's visible within filters, and it lives within user inboxes).

Let's go into more detail about how companies can take advantage of the unified traffic framework with utility marketing.

FILTERS

Filters are generally the highest-value properties online. They make usable a chaotic and complex digital world of unlimited choice, with users associating them with a specific "do/find something" need.

To really get a handle on their influence and power, let's take a step back. In the brick-and-mortar world, products, space, and choice are limited. A typical Barnes & Noble bookstore only holds about a hundred thousand unique titles on its shelves; movies must compete for time across a universe of just thirty-nine thousand screens; a supermarket—even the largest mega, super, ultra Walmart—still has finite boundaries. And in all of these cases, the decision of what to showcase falls to the retailer. Executives at Barnes & Noble sift through masses of books before deciding which will be present in-store, and which ones will get how much shelf space. AMC decides what movies will be available to local audiences. Walmart executives carefully plan exactly which products will be stocked at various outposts. Then if all of these businesses reside in the same mall, another barrier exists—the mall's governing body decides which stores get to be within its boundaries. These limits and the choices they force on the ecosystem aren't a bad thing. They present people with just enough options to find anything they could need and few enough options to make the selection simple and manageable.

The Internet is dramatically different because e-retailers stock warehouses full of every movie, every book, and every other object that a consumer could think of. A single business can sell millions upon millions of products. After all, there's no shelf space to conserve. They can promote each with just kilobytes of their massive server space. Then because there is no mall, no real estate zones, no barriers to entry, these big brand-name stores compete with every store—mom-and-pop shops from around the world are in the same "mall" with Barnes & Noble and Walmart. And these lesser known stores can also sell an unlimited number of items. On the Internet, there is no natural limit to consumer choice. And because of this, users must rely on trusted authorities to sift through what's available and present them with a valuable, small portion that's likely to meet their needs.

That's what filters do. They sift through masses of information to provide users with a digestible selection of products or sites that are likely to satisfy the relevant need. In short, they direct users to the information they want.

This is what Google does so well. Users can go to that famous, unadulterated white search box to meet nearly every possible need. For Google the brand, this "brand utility" has been the ultimate win. Its role elevates it to a level of prominence above and beyond what any other site could easily reach. If a site doesn't show up in a Google search, users would have almost no way of knowing it exists.

Google may be the king filter, but there are many more. I go directly to Amazon.com when I want to find a book; I go to YouTube when I'm looking for that funny video; I go to Kayak when I want a cheap flight; I go to Digg or Reddit when I want to read top-of-mind news and information. All of these search/find tools fit the definition. They sort through grand universes of information, produce a limited array that will most likely meet the need of their users, and become household names in the process.

While being a filter is an incredible marketing opportunity, it's incredibly difficult to become one. Competition is extremely tight. The more an existing filter meets user needs, the stronger the association between the filter and the task becomes in the users' minds—they really, really fall in love with the site or application, and are highly likely to use it again whenever the need comes up. Then they often evangelize it to all of their friends. For this reason, great filters that get traction tend to grow quickly and take the lead in a category. It also means that there are very few players in any market, because generally only one brand can be successful in creating an association around a certain set of tasks in the minds of consumers. The result is a phenomenon where when a company such as eBay or Amazon wins, everyone else loses.

DESTINATION

The next best thing to being a filter is to be a destination*—a Web site, application, or Facebook page that gets direct traffic because users associate it with a clear task.

The primary way brands become destinations is by creating "brand utility" in the form of content: articles, videos, blogs, Twitter streams, and other forms of communication that together function to turn the brand into its own media property—also called private label media. Of-

---

* Filters are starting to encroach on the destination territory. Many people now go to Google for the weather and movie times, not just for its search results. But a destination is inherently different from a filter because its business model is about satisfying users through its own single brand more than leading users to products or information run by a third-party company.

ten, we think of online media as falling into two buckets: "professional" digital media properties, which pay their writers, and social media properties, consisting of consumers who post videos and other content for free. Now, companies are increasingly creating and managing their own editorial content. By providing valuable content, the brand is in essence offering users a free service. Users will think of the brand when they want to find a recipe, learn how to fix a toilet, play games, or decide what to wear and not just on the potentially infrequent occasions that they're shopping for the brand's products. Then users will do what they do whenever they land upon a usable, valuable product: they'll tell their friends and family about it. Bloggers will link to it in their own blogs. These destinations can quickly become part of the fabric of a user's digital experience.

I'll give you an example. Not long ago, my wife and I had dinner at a friend's house. We raved about the meal, and when we got home we were greeted with a friendly e-mail from our hosts that contained links to the recipes. None of the links were to epicurious, the Food Network, or Allrecipes.com. Rather every link pointed to KraftRecipes.com. A quick look at traffic statistics confirmed my suspicions: KraftRecipes.com is one of the largest recipe sites on the Web.

Other companies are making similar efforts:

- General Mills' BettyCrocker.com, which provides recipes and cooking tips, is roughly the same size, in terms of traffic, as KraftRecipes.com.

- Lego.com, which features a wide array of original online games, attracts 1.5 million visitors per month.

- Johnson & Johnson owns the top global interactive parenting network, BabyCenter.com.

- Lowe's features a plethora of articles and videos on DIY home repair.

- Juicy Couture, Donna Karan, Tory Burch, and many other luxury brands are getting into the act with blogs, editorial-style photos, and even extras like city guides and brand social networks.

All of these companies looked at their marketing budgets and decided it would make more sense to own than to rent, to become a true utility rather than a promotional sponsor. Instead of renting more space for banner ads or sponsoring a takeover of a high-traffic site, these companies decided to be the valuable utility themselves, to use their advertising budget as a direct investment in their own growth. What's more, these sites often cost less to generate audience impressions and can result in higher audience engagement as well as more brand loyalty. These sites are governed by a radically different business model from the traditional marketing one that has the potential to transform the digital advertising business and how consumers interact with brands.

FILTER RECIPIENTS

It's nearly impossible to wake up one day and decide to become a mainstream filter. It's also not an easy task to turn a brand known for toys, packaged goods, or leather purses into a media company. But every company successful in digital media promotes itself as a filter recipient, basically making sure it shows up in the path of users looking to "do or find something" by prominently appearing in relevant search results. This is an integral way of introducing an existing destination to new users, and for some brands, it's their lifeblood.

Launched in 1997, About.com was a success story from the first dot-com boom. The company built a strong reputation as a go-to source by building a collection of Web sites, each dedicated to a topic and written by expert "guides." Nearly any topic you can imagine had its own page and resident expert. In those early days of widespread Internet adoption, it became a *destination* for people interested in learning all sorts of information. About 75 percent of About.com's traffic came direct, while just 25 percent of visitors found it through links from one of the fledgling search engines.

But as search engines gained prominence, About.com's position as a destination was thwarted. Users stopped thinking of About.com as the answer to all "find something/do something" inquiries and started to rely on search engines for that instead. This meant About.com could no longer attract traffic just by being its own brand name. Rather, it needed to optimize its site to show up prominently in search results.

The strategic decision to optimize its visibility in search engines and evolve with user behavior was About.com's saving grace. As a result of its efforts, the way users found the site completely reversed: just 25 percent of the visitors were entering direct and 75 percent were entering on topic pages via search engines. It became a full-fledged filter recipient, surviving through the traffic sent to it from Google and other prominent filters. In 2005, About.com was purchased by The New York Times Company. And guess what? About.com now gets more traffic than NYTimes.com even though no one thinks of going there first. Today the site ranks as one of the top thirty most visited on the Web. The value of the information it provides in conjunction with its powerful filter recipient strategy has buoyed it to an incredible level of success.

Being a filter recipient, while easier than becoming a filter or a destination, is not a risk-free way to embrace utility marketing. About.com pretty much lives and dies by Google—when Google's search volume increases, so does About.com's traffic; when Google's search traffic slows, About.com's traffic dips. Therein lies the beauty and vulnerability of being a filter recipient. You just ride along the ebbing and flowing wave of your host. That's not to say you don't have to protect your rank. There is a risk that one day a filter will begin pointing traffic to someone else's site. For this reason, it's vital that filter recipients continually battle to improve their rankings.

Amazon.com also has a flurry of dependent filter recipients. Ever heard of Geroy's? Probably not. Geroy's is a locally owned home-improvement store located in Roseau, Minnesota, a town of sixteen thousand just a couple of miles south from the Canadian border. As a small store, there was no way it could compete online with the likes of Walmart, Home Depot, Lowe's, and others. So it made the logical decision to market and sell its products by leveraging filters such as Amazon, eBay, and DoItBest.com, an online store representing more than four thousand independently owned hardware stores and DIY centers. And it hit it out of the park. Geroy's receives about two thousand reviews a month on Amazon, which is likely a fraction of the items it actually sells—not bad for a small store.

There's a whole world of companies that have hitched their wagons to Amazon. Search for Michael Lewis's book *The Big Short* and you'll get ninety-seven different sellers offering new versions of the hardcover. You can buy it from Amazon for $16.63 or a seller called "treebeardbooks" for $16.29. Treebeardbooks may not be a household name, but it's been reviewed on Amazon a little more than twenty-six thousand times in the past year. Granted, winning by price isn't often a moneymaking option. Amazon filter recipients likely run on extremely low margins, but with traffic driven by Amazon, it's likely their volume of transactions can keep them in the black.

BECOMING A RELATED LINK

Getting listed prominently by Google or Amazon is just one way to gain traffic from existing digital properties. Another way is to have a link to your destination placed within the path of your target user's online task. Imagine your user is at a destination shopping for computer monitors, when she sees a link that she believes will lead her to more information she wants to know, for example, a site that demystifies all of the esoteric technical specifications. So she clicks on it. And then she sees another relevant link, this time perhaps to a deal on a monitor, so she clicks again. As long as the link is directly related to the user's immediate interests, she's likely to click on it.

When a brand builds its utility through content creation and private label media, related links are a primary way it attracts valuable traffic. In fact, it's how lots of the traditional media properties attract visitors. Often these related links come from content partnerships or curation by editors. For example, Reuters is a well-known news service, but few people think of going straight to its Web site to find the latest news. Rather, other news sites that don't have their own stable of high-quality journalists link to Reuters' articles. This is how Reuters gets most of its traffic.

This type of relationship is woven throughout nearly every news site you visit. Investing Web site Investopedia.com gets a boost in its traffic through links in Yahoo!'s finance pages. WashingtonPost.com usually receives traffic from the Drudge Report, which links to its news stories. Sometimes these content-sharing deals are based on an editor's discretion; other times it's a formal, contractual partnership. Either way both parties benefit. One gets to appear as though it has gobs of content, even if it barely creates any of its own, and the other gets traffic from being related to the user's search at hand. Blogs and social networks are similar venues for link sharing.

PAYING FOR RELEVANCE

Our conversation so far about filter recipients and related links has been based on the assumption that the link placement is gained somewhat organically, through natural inclusion in search results or articles. For example, the Google algorithm says, "Hey, that's a high quality site relevant to the search, I should list it toward the top." Or an editor or blogger says, "This is a good piece of content. I'm going to link to it because it'll make mine stronger." To a degree, both of these tactics rely on good luck. Brands, however, don't have to rely on luck. They can buy placement too, through sponsored search results, display ads that are directly relevant to the user, or textual links adjacent to a related article. As long as the advertising one buys is truly related to the user's task at hand and the user's mindset, it will likely perform well and drive traffic to your destination—indeed, it's among the only kind of advertising that's been proven to be effective.* However, a word of caution: all traffic is not created equal. You might get a monster boost in traffic from a

---

* Saying that digital advertising is completely ineffective is a bit of a simplification; the topic of effective digital advertising could easily be the subject of an entire book. Suffice it to say that advertising that is highly contextually relevant to a user's task is effective, along with ads that are behaviorally targeted, because they're consistent with user needs. On the opposite extreme, there are some digital environments that enable "old school" storytelling to a captive audience—for example, a video advertisement playing within a sitcom on Hulu—and these have similarly been proven to be effective. But everything in the middle is of questionable value.

sponsored Google listing, but it won't attract as many seriously interested, potential new users to your destination as going the organic route. The more your destination can be introduced to new users as being of genuine value and utility, the more traction it will generate in the market. Paid advertising can undermine the message that a brand is providing a selfless utility for the good of its users who are simply trying to do or find something.

TELL ME WHAT'S NEW: GETTING INTO THE INBOX

In August 2010, Americans spent 41.1 billion minutes on Facebook as opposed to 39.8 billion minutes on Google, according to data from comScore. It was the first time the social network had passed the search engine to become the most used site in the country. In early 2011, Twitter was adding 460,000 new users per day, for a total of 200 million users.

These figures highlight the growing importance of the other reason people go online: to get new information from people and about subjects they care about. Millions of people check at least one of three inboxes—e-mail, Facebook, and Twitter—several times a day to get updates from their friends and read other messages that have been sent to them. And let's not forget about other inboxes: mobile text messages, push notifications on mobile phones, RSS feeds, and instant messages.

To get into the inbox, brands should not try to create a new inbox themselves. Existing inboxes are so deeply entrenched in the lives of users that it's nearly impossible to dethrone them. And users are already overloaded with too many inboxes to monitor, so it's hard to motivate them to check someplace new. The best thing marketers can do is leverage the inboxes that now exist. There are two approaches:

1. **Show up in inboxes.** Here the goal is to get users to sign up for your e-mail list or Twitter feed, or to become a fan of the brand on Facebook. This allows marketers to send messages directly to their audiences.

2. **Go viral.** Here the objective is to convince users to send their friends a message about the brand and a link to its destination. Usually the message asks friends to watch, read, or participate in something. This is the core mechanism that's driven virtually every large Internet marketing success story.

GETTING IN THE INBOX BY GIVING VALUE

Users allow you to send messages to their inbox for the same reason users will forward a message—something of value is being shared. The Internet is full of businesses that are fundamentally about giving something away for free, and then monetizing the resulting audience by selling them something that's paid or selling that audience to a third party through advertising. That's the premise behind Google and Facebook—in exchange for using a great free search engine or social network, those companies will expose you to advertising. And it's the premise of Web applications such as Dropbox and Evernote, which provide free document sharing services with for-pay premium features just a click away. These are examples of true user-first utility marketing: they build brand loyalty by generating (free) usefulness to the user, and the money follows.

Getting direct access to the user's inbox is no different. Users need something of value—something free—for them to agree to receive your messages in such a personal, protected place. But give them this, and you'll reap incredible dividends. The inbox is the one place on the Internet where a true captive audience exists. If I send you a message I know you'll see it—assuming I don't abuse this privilege and get thrown into the spam folder.

Brands use two proven approaches for accessing to user inboxes, whether it is e-mail, Twitter, or Facebook:

- **Deals**: Consumers love deals, especially during more difficult economic times. Access to coupons, special offers, exclusive opportunities, and every other promotional trick in the book reliably encourages sign-up. It's the force behind everything from Starbucks' 1.5 million-follower Twitter feed to JetBlue's massive e-mail list for fare alerts. Offer discounts and the consumers who think favorably of you will soon sign up for your Twitter feed, Facebook page, or e-mail list.

- **Content**: Discounts and products are not the only things to give away; content can be just as effective. Consumers will sign up to receive compelling content, especially content that really resonates with their needs and is consistent with the brand. S. C. Johnson's RightAtHome.com initiative is a good example. It's a private-label media play combining a Web site with e-mail newsletters that get sent to millions of women each month. Then there's Red Bull's Facebook page. It has nearly twenty million fans that agree to have Red Bull post to their news feed, all for great extreme sports videos.

Of course, the best deals and content are inherently "viral"—they're regularly and fervently shared by users to other users. Witness the success of Groupon, or famous viral campaigns such as Burger King's Subservient Chicken and the Old Spice Man. Whether it's a really good deal or amazing content, if users find it has value, be it a bout of cheek-aching laughter or 50 percent off a spa service, people will share it, and that's the ultimate win when it comes to inbox marketing.

THE INTEGRATED UTILITY MARKETING SOLUTION

The most successful utility marketers combine all of the elements of the unified traffic framework into a single marketing solution. A destination is created that can attract direct traffic, can be optimized to rank toward the top in search results, can be set up to directly message its audience, and has enough utility to users that other destinations link to it and users refer it to each other, thereby landing in more inboxes. The National Association of Realtors' HouseLogic initiative is a small example of this integrated approach.

The National Association of Realtors, with around 1.1 million members, is the largest trade organization in the United States. Founded in 1908, the NAR offers training and accreditation to people working in real estate and lobbies politicians across the country for the interests of its membership.

The NAR recognized early on that the Internet's power to make real-estate listings more available to the public could threaten the livelihoods of professional real-estate agents. So the association responded by creating Realtor.com, a heavily trafficked Web site known for having the most property listings on the Internet.

More recently, the association decided to use the Internet to forge a direct connection with homeowners and homebuyers. "We are, like many trade organizations, a political organization, and our objective is to shape the legislative and regulatory climate in which real estate is transacted," says Anne Feder, a digital executive at the NAR. "The challenge that our leadership saw is that while we have always been effective in that realm and we're certainly a major player, there are a lot of people out there with the same money and legislative capabilities that we have." The NAR's point of difference and key to success in influencing Congress could be grassroots support from homeowners.

But rather than launch a site aimed at homeowners that preached the often abstract importance of the NAR's legislative issues, the NAR decided to give homeowners something that would more clearly, directly affect their lives: a site with content targeted toward helping Americans maintain, protect, and increase the values of their homes. Then, when political issues came along for which the NAR wanted consumer support, they would just have to ask their existing loyal audience of homeowners.

The result, launched in February 2010, is HouseLogic.com, a site that includes articles and news developed by the NAR's editorial team as well as a first-rate group of professional writers who also pen articles for publications including *The Wall Street Journal, Real Simple,* and *This Old House.* Topics ranged from tax planning, finance, and insurance to seasonal home improvement advice. Users who register on the site can create to-do lists, set project reminders, and customize the site for their type of home and where they live. If a registrant likely qualifies for a tax credit in return for replacing their heating and cooling systems, the site will let them know. "People have a need for this information, the quality is quite high, and the bylines are by people who have been writing about housing and buying and selling for top-tier publications for a long time," says Feder.

At the same time, the NAR has positioned HouseLogic content as a value for its core members, Realtors. They want to be seen not only as agents of transaction, but as trusted advisors. Because HouseLogic is about making smart decisions about your home through a financial values lens and because it's connected with the NAR and its Realtor members, it helps shape perceptions of what services Realtors might have to offer. In addition, the NAR offered its Realtor base free HouseLogic content to put on their own Web sites. Previously, a typical Realtor would pay an average of $400 a year for canned content. So when HouseLogic offered Realtors this utility, the community naturally embraced it. In expectation of this, HouseLogic made all of its content easily sharable to all of its million members through a technology solution that used qualities of concentric organization and disposable technology. The association built a companion product that offered Realtor members HouseLogic content in easily distributable modules that would allow them to post it on their sites, Facebook and Twitter, and even make handouts.

This type of content syndication also functioned as a marketing play. Suddenly the HouseLogic brand was present on seller sites around the country. Then to further support the site's brand, HouseLogic produced "buzzworthy" articles designed to spark conversation and encourage sharing from one user to another. These buzz articles, as well as the more traditional home maintenance fare, were regularly promoted on House-Logic's Facebook page and Twitter feed, through link-sharing sites like Digg and Reddit, and through paid search campaigns and banner ads. Additionally, its articles show up naturally in the results of related Google searches.

With all of this power behind it—the leveraging of Realtor-customer relationships, related-link placement and buying, social media outreach, and most of all the foundation of real value the site offers visitors—its traffic has soared. During its first several months, 3.5 million users directly visited the site and tens of millions of people have been exposed to the brand by seeing links and snippets of content posted via Facebook, Twitter, and blogs.

Nine months later, after the site had its feet in the water, it was time to try promoting NAR's public policy issues. In October 2010, HouseLogic and the NAR launched Operation Home Relief. The NAR wanted to lobby for more government support for mortgage modification and other measures to help people remain in their homes. So HouseLogic and the NAR teamed up with USA Cares, a charity that helps provide financial assistance to military personnel in danger of losing their homes. As part of their joint Operation Home Relief campaign, HouseLogic posted a series of articles on individual military families facing foreclosure. This was linked to the campaign's page on Facebook Causes, which called for support for these families. For everyone who joined the cause, House-Logic pledged to donate one dollar to USA Cares, up to $131,000. Word spread quickly, fueled by NAR's member network, press coverage, and support from celebrities such as Jessica Simpson, and later Alyssa Milano, who voluntarily joined the pledge. Within the first twenty days, twenty thousand people had joined, making it one of the fastest growing campaigns ever on Facebook Causes.

All in all, HouseLogic has provided a higher return on investment than would have been possible with a traditional campaign. "The NAR has a thirty to forty million dollar branding campaign using TV, radio, print, online. But HouseLogic is doing something different, as now we have an audience of hundreds of thousands of people who come to the Web site every month and ten thousand signed up right now through e-mail," Feder says.

To get the most from its dollar, the NAR built a valuable brand utility and an entire marketing ecosystem around it that ultimately touched all levels of the united traffic framework. To build your own user-centric utility marketing campaign, start with the development of one or more destinations based on a brand utility that addresses an existing need of your target users. This anchors the utility marketing ecosystem. The destination can be one Web site, several Web sites, a domain directly related to the brand, or one that's completely separate. It can be the company's

Facebook page; it can even be a mobile app. What matters is that the experience meets user needs and as a result it has a chance at becoming a destination—that place users know to go to first when they want to solve a particular task. When this happens, a direct and lasting relationship is formed between user and brand.

Then the experience must be introduced to new users and ultimately generate traffic by becoming a filter recipient and a related link. To become a filter recipient, the site must be optimized for search engines to find it. To get "related link" traffic from other destinations, the utility can be pitched to bloggers and the press, promoted on social networks, and distributed via partnerships with other destinations. The result should be lots of links around the web pointing to your brand utility.

Then the initiative needs a way to access user inboxes. This means putting in place a plan that persuades people to voluntarily receive your communications and/or structuring the experience so users are likely to share it with friends. This could mean encouraging users to sign up to vote for Pepsi Refresh Projects, and then coaxing them to tell their friends about it. Or in the case of HouseLogic, it was about producing buzzworthy and useful content that people signed up to receive via e-mail or updates on their social networks. For an added boost, you can work to get people who visit your destination to tell others about it, for example by asking someone to "e-mail a friend" or "like" the page. The overarching goal here is to gain access to more and more user inboxes.

Therein lies the formula for the most effective user-centric marketing, a single digital experience that places itself in the direct path of a user looking to accomplish a task. It takes advantage of the whole united traffic framework: it's a destination, a filter recipient, and related link, and it gets access to the inbox through direct messaging and by social networking. But none of this will work if the destination is not designed to provide users with a solution to their task. At the foundation of all user behavior are two qualities: unlimited choice and the intention to satisfy a particular need. To compel them to choose to be exposed to your marketing messages, you must offer them a tool or a service that solves their need, what I've called a brand utility. Then as the user takes advantage of your utility, they're being favorably exposed to your brand messaging and actually engaging with your brand—a feat nearly unattainable by captive messaging. As seen in the rise of Google, Facebook, Mint, Amazon, and other leaders in user-centricity, their utility is so strong and their integration into the united traffic framework so comprehensive, they have rarely relied on traditional advertising to build their vast markets of loyal users.

All the utility marketing in the world, however, won't persuade people to buy your products if your setup for online sales is lacking. Your digital ecosystem, whether designed for e-commerce or to drive offline sales, must meet a combination of four basic user needs—trust, convenience, price, and fun—in order to convert users into customers. That's what we'll discuss next.

CHAPTER SUMMARY: UTILITY MARKETING

Market Insights

- The traditional model of advertising—telling stories to a captive audience—is not effective online for a simple reason: audiences have infinite choice and they don't have to be exposed to your message if they don't want to. Audiences have generally become blind to banner advertising, and there are limited forums to expose a captive viewer to a thirty-second video spot. The only venue for truly effective captive messaging is user in-boxes—a venue that can be very hard to access.

- Twenty years of digital media use has revealed that people use the Internet in predictable ways—as defined by the unified traffic framework. Users approach the Internet with one of two motivations: either to accomplish something or to find out what's new. The need to know what's new drives them to the in-box—be it e-mail, SMS, their Twitter feed, or Facebook newsfeed. Accomplishing something drives them to a place that they associate in their mind with this task. This can be a filter, which helps users find the final destination for their problem, or it can be an actual destination. Users flow through these three areas—inbox, filters, and destinations—through referrals and user-to-user messaging.

Strategic Imperatives

- Marketing must be in the service of the user. It must help users solve their problems. This approach—utility marketing—allows companies to communicate brand messaging to an audience that is actively engaging with them.

- Utility marketing involves execution of a program that uses all levers of the united traffic framework to build awareness: a destination is created, which users can associate with accomplishing a specific task; by design, it drives traffic from a filter (for example, Google); by interacting with the destination, users allow the brand to send relevant messages to their inboxes (which can be e-mail or posts to their Facebook wall); and it has elements that cause users and other destinations to tell others about it, creating additional referral traffic. Pepsi Refresh and HouseLogic are examples of large and small effective initiatives that fit this model.

- In the context of the unified traffic framework and a user-first approach to marketing, paid advertising is most effective in the form of paid referrals from filters and destinations that directly relate to the user's task at hand and mindset.

6

TCPF Sales

Turn Users into Customers by Addressing Their Four Basic Needs:
Trust, Convenience, Price, and Fun

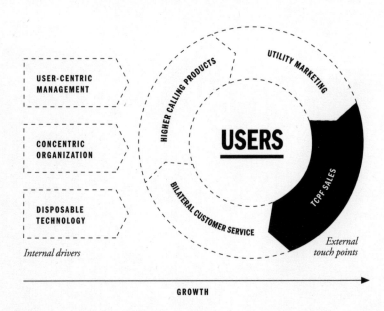

Today's user obviously demands the ability to not just shop, but to purchase things online; online shopping is the vital link that turns (nonpaying) users into (paying) customers. As a result, e-commerce has become a critical part of every company's strategy. It has permeated the thinking behind every business, even those with products so mundane that online shopping would seem to be a chore (for example, aspirin or chewing gum), or for products so complex that personal interaction would seem required to make a sale (for example, financial services products). The question is not whether a company should be selling online. The question is how. Because if you're not selling online, a competitor will, winning business from you in the process.

As is the case with other functional areas of business, a user-first approach to selling will most likely position a firm for success.

WHY USERS BUY

Successful user-first selling begins with the obvious question: why do users buy from one place instead of somewhere else? User behavior is straightforward: they'll buy from the cheapest, most convenient, and trustworthy place, unless they're in the mindset of shopping as a leisure activity, in which case entertainment and fun is a big part of the mix. When a purchase is on the horizon, users quickly run through a mental exercise—balancing trust, convenience, price, and fun (TCPF)—to decide where to shop and buy. TCPF thinking can vary by individual. Some people will pay more to buy something that's convenient; others will buy from a less-than-reputable source if it means getting a good deal. It also varies with an individual's current mindset. One day convenience may be more important to me; another day I may have more free time and want to shop at a place that's fun. And the thought process applies to physical stores, as well as debating whether I buy from an online or brick-and-mortar retailer. For example, is it more important for me to have the convenience of buying at the local grocer, or is it worth it to drive twenty minutes to get the cost savings of buying bulk at Costco? Or do I just buy from Fresh Direct?

In the early days of the Internet, when it was time for users to make the decision about where to buy, the physical store generally won the TCPF comparison battle, because Internet retailers hadn't yet earned trust. Consumers wouldn't trust online buying for something expensive, something they had to try on, or something they wanted to talk to a salesperson about. Among the many genius moves of Jeff Bezos, founder, president, and CEO of Amazon, was pioneering e-commerce by focusing on the easiest possible product in which the trust problem could be overcome. A book title is a known entity. No trying on, not hugely expensive, not something you'd talk to a salesperson about. All Bezos had to do was convince consumers that Amazon would indeed ship them the requested book and charge their credit card for the right amount. He made most consumer trust issues a moot point.

Fast forward two decades and we've seen increasingly complicated and expensive products and services make significant inroads in e-commerce. From diamonds to mobile service, real estate to car shopping, categories that the pundits once said would never sell online are now being regularly bought and sold via the Internet. Indeed, current trends suggest it's only a matter of time before users conduct the majority of their purchases in the digital space.

So how does an individual company succeed in selling its wares online? It either needs a compelling story across all four TCPF drivers, or more commonly, it needs to prioritize a specific component of TCPF and make the decision that it will only appeal to users with consistent needs: for example, by just focusing on being the price leader, or by placing an extreme emphasis on convenience. Let's examine each component in detail:

TRUST

For many users, trust is a make-it-or-break-it attribute when deciding where to purchase a product—particularly for the decision about whether to buy online versus offline. When I visit a store and consider purchasing a product, the trust factor is high: I can touch the product, see the *actual, exact* item I'm buying, not a visual representation of it, and talk to a salesperson. If all else fails, I have the comfort of knowing that I can always return it. Sure, hucksterism still exists, but by and large physical shopping is a trustworthy experience.

Digital stores, on the other hand, are lacking many of the "trustworthy" attributes of physical stores: I can't touch the product; I can't see the real thing I'm buying; and I can't get the level of human service required to get comfortable since there's rarely someone for me to talk to. To compound matters, I have to trust that my credit card number won't get stolen and what I think I'm buying will actually get sent to me.

Amazon solved the biggest trust barrier of all—it proved that e-commerce actually works. It's built a brand where users completely trust the fulfillment component of the transaction (credit card payment, reliable shipping and returns, etc.). But Amazon is not alone in earning user trust. Indeed, all great innovations—and big successes—in e-commerce have come from companies that have understood the nuances surrounding user trust and convinced consumers to give them a chance. Fresh Direct did it for groceries, persuading consumers it can be trusted to select and deliver fresh produce; Cars Direct did it for buying a car, showing price is no barrier to trust; Zappos did it for shoes, solving trust with a generous return policy; and Airbnb has done it for the most risky of transactions, renting out a stranger's home for use during a vacation—where outright fraud seems most likely, and the consequences of the deception (a ruined vacation) seems most severe.

The number-one question a company looking to build a successful e-commerce business must resolve is: "How can I make sure my users are comfortable buying my products and services online?" The answer lies in a three-step process of standardization, simplification, and amplification:

1. **Standardization:** The product and service must be standardized enough so users trust what they're buying online without seeing the product firsthand or having an expert explain it to them. Books—what Amazon opened its business with—are the ultimate in standardization, but standardization drives virtually everything we purchase online—even legal services. LegalZoom, an online legal document and filing service provider founded in 2001, captured a lot of the low-end legal services market by standardizing dozens of routine legal needs. If someone wants a living will, for example, rather than finding a lawyer and

going through a whole legal process, he or she can visit
LegalZoom.com, fill out a form, and get one for just $39. If
a couple wants to file for an uncontested divorce, it can pay
$299 (not including any court fees), fill out some forms, and
be done with it. LegalZoom has turned an intricate, often
individualized service into a simple product that anyone can
understand, thereby enabling e-commerce transactions in
the legal field. Imagine a lawyer trying to sell online legal
services for $100 an hour—impossible!

2. **Simplification:** Once the product is standardized, the next
   step is simplifying the exact price and offer so users understand exactly what they're going to be charged. LegalZoom
   perfected this as well. Creating a living will with a real lawyer is an uncertain cost—who knows how many billable
   hours it will take? But LegalZoom's living will offer is finite
   and clear—$39 for the basic version and $49 for the comprehensive version—and the Web site offers a simple checklist to explain the differences.

   Key to simplification is reassuring the user that the
   prices seen online really are the best they can get. I recently
   switched cable television providers from TimeWarner to
   RCN. But when I went to the RCN Web site to check
   available offers, I didn't trust that I was getting the best
   deal. So I called them up, haggled with the customer-
   service representative for a few minutes, and felt much
   better about the price. I'm not the only user who feels
   this way. Online sales of telecommunications services are
   fairly low as an industry, and cable companies have massive
   call center expenses. But if the RCN Web site had given
   me confidence in the specific price and package it offered
   online, and guaranteed that the deal was the best I could
   get—maybe even better than through calling them—I
   would have happily saved time and bought online. I'm sure
   other users would do the same.

3. **Amplification:** Once transactions are standardized and simplified, users start to trust buying the product online. But the number of transactions won't quickly or easily scale without positive word of mouth. Hearing about users' good experiences makes other people much more comfortable partaking in it themselves. For example, when I first heard of Airbnb's service that lets you rent your apartment to a complete stranger or rent a stranger's apartment, I thought you had to be crazy. But when a few people told me about their positive experiences with it, my doubts were alleviated and now I'd consider doing it too. The most successful e-commerce innovators make a point of amplifying success stories as much as they can.

CONVENIENCE

When deciding whether to shop online or in a physical store, users weigh cost and convenience. In March 2011, *New York Times* journalist Ron Lieber crystallized this decision-making process when he compared shopping at Costco for his household needs to Amazon's subscription program where items such as toilet paper are regularly sent to the home. He started by comparing prices of everything on his shopping list, such as Huggies diapers, Lubriderm lotion, and Ziploc sandwich bags, to the price of the items available through Amazon's subscription program. Costco was cheaper by about forty-three dollars. Then he factored in the time required to drive to Costco, wait in line, load the car, drive home, and unload the car—about two hours. "I happen to value two hours of my time at a lot more than the $43," Lieber wrote.

But we all know digital commerce is not always the most convenient choice. For the most part, it satisfies the impulse for an immediate purchase—checking out via e-commerce, particularly on a site where you've saved your credit card information, can take less time and effort than tying your shoelaces. But it fails to satisfy the impulse of using the product *right now* thanks to the inevitable delay caused by shipping. If Lieber ordered his items from Amazon, he was still going to have to wait a few days for his Huggies and Ziploc bags to arrive (of course, with the subscription service, orders after the initial one would be automatically processed and shipped). And often online shopping gets complicated when you have to buy many different things from many different sites. This realistically means multiple shipping fees and multiple orders to track. It can be more convenient, if you're buying lots of various items, to do so at a mall, where all of the stores are in close proximity. Then in the case of clothing or shoes, it can be a hassle to order and return items via snail mail or UPS rather than just driving to the department store and trying them on. While the above issues may seem obvious and trivial, the point is that solving for convenience demands thinking carefully about the real user experience. It's about making the user's life easier in the broadest context, understanding his or her full environment and lifestyle and how your sales offering fits into the equation.

This means that for companies looking to conquer e-commerce, the notion of convenience goes back to a user-first perspective: what can be done to ensure that it's as easy as possible to buy? How can we remove the friction to purchase? Amazon solves this quandary with things like its seventy-nine-dollar-a-year prime membership that offers free two-day shipping. For FreshDirect and Drugstore.com, it's saving customer shopping lists so users don't need to hunt for regularly purchased items each time they want to buy. For others it's about selling products via mobile apps and Facebook—because true convenience means allowing ordering from anywhere, and not forcing people to visit your Web site.

Most people don't think of food as being a big seller online, but in recent years, digital food ordering has become big business. The top three U.S. pizza delivery chains—Pizza Hut, Domino's Pizza, and Papa John's International—have been innovators in online ordering, rolling out a variety of options in recent years in an arms race for the biggest slice of a growing market of digital customers. It's therefore no surprise that this arms race would extend to the mobile sphere. Released in July 2009, Pizza Hut's iPhone app was designed to be easy, fast, and fun—

and it's exactly that. It takes less than a minute to go through the ordering process. The choices are clear, the path to purchase so simple a toddler could do it, it stores pizzas you've ordered in the past for easy reordering, and it uses engaging mobile functionalities such as asking you to shake the phone to cover wings in sauce and inviting you to play a car racing game. (No, this aspect doesn't add convenience, but it adds fun—a vital differentiator to be discussed shortly.) Imagine a college student getting out of an evening class and thinking about what he wants for dinner. He considers stopping by the supermarket on the way back to his apartment or maybe going to Subway for a sandwich. But then he remembers he has Pizza Hut's mobile app on his iPhone. All he has to do is pull out his phone, fire up the Pizza Hut app, quickly build a pizza, and hit send. It should arrive at his apartment around the time he gets there. Pizza Hut has just made a sale it might not have otherwise. By the fall of 2010, the app had been downloaded two million times. And in 2011, Pizza Hut introduced Android and iPad apps as well. These tools are the foundation of a broader strategy of removing the barriers to transactions, so the impulse to eat pizza can quickly be translated into a pizza at the user's door. Convenience is paramount to getting the sale.

As the growth of smart-phone use continues, we're seeing mobile apps offer convenient, automated services for personal transactions that had traditionally been conducted in person. Walgreens pharmacy, for example, has launched iPhone and Android apps that allow users to capture a prescription bar code to order a refill; when it's ready for pick-up, the users get an alert via text. Users can also refill prescriptions by accessing their account history. Other features include flu shot scheduling, photo ordering, a map of nearby locations using GPS, and the ability to build a shopping list from the current weekly circular. CVS has a similar iPhone app, and Walmart has a mobile optimized website. Today, even though the digitization of medical records and personal privacy can still elicit a lively debate, a pharmacy that doesn't offer the convenience of a mobile program risks losing customers.

The incredible convenience of a transaction, being just a click away in the pockets of users on the go anywhere on earth 24/7, is why companies in the Digital Leadership Set think about e-commerce across the full digital ecosystem, not just a Web site.

At its foundation, however, convenience in e-commerce is inherently about user-friendly Web site design. If someone finds it hard to complete a purchase, that transaction becomes extremely inconvenient, and when that happens there's a big risk that purchase won't be made.

American Airlines is a case in point. On May 18, 2009, user interface designer Dustin Curtis voluntarily redesigned AA.com with an open letter to the company. "Recently, I had the horrific displeasure of booking a flight on your Web site, aa.com. The experience was so bad that I vowed never to fly your airline again. . . . If I was running a company with the distinction and history of American Airlines, I would be embarrassed—no ashamed—to have a Web site with a customer experience as terrible as the one you have now." The site was unarguably lacking focus. There were three chock-full columns of small text, ads, and three competing levels of global navigation. There was simply too much information on the home page and minimal clarity on how users could use the site to meet their needs. It genuinely looked more like an internal corporate system than one tailored to customers. Curtis redesigned the site with a single focus of booking travel and limited to the options to "explore destinations," "your reservations," "online check-in," and "flight status." It had one pretty photo of Fiji and a weather advisory for the northeastern United States. It clearly addressed a traveler's basic needs— quite an improvement.

Soon after Curtis posted his work, a user-experience designer at American Airlines responded. "The group running AA.com consists of at least 200 people spread out amongst many different groups, including, for example, QA, product planning, business analysis, code development, site operations, project planning, and user experience. We have a lot of people touching the site, and a lot more with their own vested interests in how the site presents its content and functionality." It was a problem that good user-centric management and concentric organization would have easily solved. The American Airlines designer was fired for his candor.

A year and a half later, however, American Airlines was able to launch a new, significantly more easy-to-use Web site. Among the improvements were: centering the site in a user's browser, enlarging the page width to increase readability, presenting more clearly prioritized navigational choices, offering users the option to select their preferred country and language, and allowing users to go back and forth between pages while booking a flight—in the past users were forced to start over. How inconvenient is that? While there are complainers everywhere online, responses from critics and users included many positive sentiments such as, "a vast improvement" and "very well done." One commenter on the site primed for negative comments, crankyflier.com, said, "It may not be perfect, but it's a hell of a lot better than the old one." And another said, "It now looks like a Web site designed this century." With a Web site that's more intuitive for users and designed to better help them meet their needs, it's easier and more convenient than ever before for users to become American Airlines customers.

Other tools in the quest to provide users with convenience are application programming interfaces (APIs) and widgets. The easier it is for developers to integrate a company's shopping experience into other sites, the wider the company's footprint is, and the more accessible the site is to consumers. For example, Amazon has an API that lets other Web sites display Amazon product search, product information, and customer reviews. Then for any purchases initiated through these elements, the referring site receives a 15 percent cut. Best Buy launched a similar API, but also allowed developers to display store location and product availability information. This is a win-win for all parties. The retailer gets to spread its e-commerce platform across the broader Web, third-party Web sites get a paycheck, and users have more opportunities to pick up that book or camera they had been meaning to buy.

Another way e-commerce retailers can offer consumers incredible convenience and add increased trust to the transaction is by truly integrating the online/offline experience. For example, they can let consumers buy online and pick up in-store, or buy online and return to a physical store. This service allows consumers to save time, while also increasing trust by allowing them to see and touch a product before completing the purchase. It also offers a price cut, as there are no shipping fees to pay. The two ways this program is implemented are by offering shipping of the item to the store or by actually having the item at the store location already for immediate pickup. Best Buy's program takes advantage of both systems. Some products are ready for pickup within forty-five minutes of when the consumer placed the order, and others must be shipped there. The convenience factor is emphasized by providing these customers with reserved front-row parking spots in select stores. Another example: Barnes & Noble offers convenience unattainable by Amazon by offering in-store pickup of books. If the product is available at a local store, a customer-service representative will hold it for the customer behind the checkout counter—all with a few clicks of the mouse. No need to wait days for a hard copy of a book and no need to hunt around aisles only to learn that the book's not in stock. Sears has also gotten kudos for its program. It adds convenience (and price differentiation) by offering a five-dollar coupon if an in-store pickup item isn't ready for the customer within five minutes.

So if your company has retail locations, present users with an integrated shopping experience, one that bridges online and offline, providing the benefits of online shopping with the advantages of in-store buying. Use the physical world—the one thing you have that your digital-only competition does not—as an asset to increase the convenience of your offering. And I said before, TCPF decisions can vary by individual and an individual's present circumstances. The more user shopping preferences your site can cater to, the more users you're likely to attract.

PRICE

Obviously price is a big driver of where users make their purchases. But as was discussed in the chapter about higher callings, attracting buyers on low price isn't often a good idea for the company. When products are standardized, as they often are in e-commerce, search engines can scan for prices on the product across a wide range of online stores. That's fabulous for users—they can choose from the lowest prices out there—

but it's terrible for businesses. It almost entirely commoditizes e-commerce sites because no matter how much time and effort went into the site's development, all the bargain-hunter sees is the low price. It's the only reason he or she clicked on the site's link. It's the only reason he or she's there, to hit the buy button. Now that could be a good thing, if the low price didn't completely wipe out the product's profit margin. But often it does. It also doesn't attract return customers. The only way this bargain hunter will come back is if next time he or she conducts a search, the same store is the lowest-cost provider. Being user-first doesn't mean lowering your prices to the point that you're not profitable. It means keeping your prices competitive, but offering users advantages for shopping with you by weighing in high on the trust, convenience, and fun factors.

Discerning shoppers who are apt to become brand loyalists and return customers will often pay a little more for trust, convenience, and a better experience. Even when Googling for a standardized product, if the site with the lowest price looks sketchy, a consumer will usually be okay with paying a little bit more for a more trustworthy experience. Amazon, for example, isn't always the cheapest in a given product category, but it is cheap enough that when the site's reliability and convenience are weighed in, it could easily be a shopper's best option. Brand amenities also come into play here. Say someone is shopping for an airline ticket. She knows she has to travel from point A to point B on particular days, so she searches the price on multiple airline sites or a comparison search engine such as Kayak.com. If one flight is significantly cheaper than the others, it won't matter if it's American or Southwest, she'll pick it. But if prices are fairly similar and she has a preferred airline (for example, she likes the television on JetBlue or is actively collecting SkyMiles on Delta), she'll pay a little extra.

Overall the key is to be aggressive on price, but it's okay if you are not the lowest. Discerning customers will often pay a little extra and plan to repeat a great experience.

FUN

Fun is the final way for a company to capture an online market from the competition. In the end, we're emotional beings. So if businesses can convince users that they *like* shopping at one Web site over another, that factor can trump all others. Trust, convenience, and price are the rational levers; fun is the emotional appeal that draws people in over and over and inspires them to share their experience with friends. Shopping in stores or walking down New York's Fifth Avenue is a fun experience for many; online shopping can also be fun, and fun can be a competitive weapon that drives e-commerce success.

Social shopping is one way e-commerce sites bring fun into the mix. Inherently shopping online is a solo activity: it involves one person at a keyboard and mouse staring at a monitor. But much of our leisure shopping, particularly that which happens in malls on evenings and weekends, gets done with friends. A leader in this arena is WetSeal.com, the Web site of the clothing store for young women. In early 2010, it launched an initiative called Shop with Friends that turns e-commerce into a virtual trip to the mall with girlfriends. Here's how it works: if a user is on WetSeal.com and wants to get advice about a blouse she's thinking of buying, she can click a button to see if any of her friends are on Facebook and then invite them to check out her selection. Through Wet Seal's interface, all of the friends can then evaluate the top and comment on it. If the original shopper wants help picking out jeans to go with it, her friends can continue to follow her around the site as she shops. This means that even if a girl has moved across the country from her best friend, the two can still go shopping together. According to Wet Seal, the Shop with Friends functionality has resulted in a 10 percent increase in sales as of March 2011. This isn't Wet Seal's only innovative and social initiative. In 2008, it launched a program where users could design outfits using Wet Seal clothing and accessories, and then share their creations with friends and other shoppers. The retailer then took this a step further by adding in-store kiosks where shoppers could scan an item to see all of the user-generated outfits in which the item was included. In December 2009, Wet Seal also released a complementary e-commerce iPhone app. As of October 2010, this program accounted for 20 percent of the revenue at

Wetseal.com, and shoppers who used the program made higher-than-average orders. For Wet Seal, bringing fun and friends into the digital shopping experience has produced incredible benefits.

But social shopping is only one way companies can use digital technology to make shopping more fun. As mentioned earlier, the Pizza Hut mobile app lets users shake the phone to cover wings in sauce and play a car racing game, all with the goal of having them order a meal on the go. Another example is Overstock.com. It adds fun to its mobile commerce app by offering users a daily "Lott-O" scratch-off card. Users can "scratch" off the ticket with a finger to uncover a daily deal such as free shipping. It incorporates innovative interactivity, a fun reveal, and a reason to open the app often. 1-800-Flowers has also been known to add fun to its mobile application. For Valentine's Day 2010, it hired Bravo's Millionaire Matchmaker, Patti Stanger, to act as a mobile love coach. She would offer users a bunch of different ways to celebrate the holiday with their loved one, and then the users could share their favorite of her suggestions with Facebook friends to see which one they should actually go forward with.

Etsy, a site where artists around the world can sell their wares to a global base of consumers, has also innovated in fun. It's easy to spend hours on the basic Etsy Web site exploring the seemingly infinite number of unique, handmade goods. But that's not as fun as this: Etsy built a system that recommends gifts based on a friend's Facebook profile. Say your friend's Facebook page says she likes Michael Jackson. The recommendation will show you a Michael Jackson pillow, baby onesie, or key chain. If she likes *The Big Lebowski*, the site presents items such as paper plates with the Dude's face or a themed bath set with bowling ball soap and a carrying bag that looks like a rug. If she likes a city like Chicago or San Francisco, a bunch of relevant items such as skyline prints and themed jewelry show up. It's an entertaining, engaging, and convenient way to surf through Etsy's products.

APPLYING TCPF TO DIFFERENT BUSINESSES

The application of TCPF can vary greatly across different business sectors. A user shopping online for a house has very different needs than one looking to buy a pizza. But this doesn't mean that when designing an e-commerce site for your product, or a site with which to sell your offline services, you have to start from scratch for your particular business. Successful online shopping experiences tend to cluster across five models that align with five different types of products and services. Each model, when implemented, will present users with a trustworthy and convenient shopping experience that puts the business well on its way to addressing the full TCPF spectrum.

The five models are illustrated here by some of the biggest brands that use them: Amazon, Zipcar, Angry Birds, Zillow, and Goldman Sachs. Each one represents a different kind of business: on the Amazon extreme we have companies that sell many items to many people; Zipcar and Angry Birds exemplify different approaches companies can take when they sell one thing to their customer base; and Zillow and Goldman Sachs represent examples of businesses that sell complex products that require a level of human service to close the deal.

MODEL #1 AMAZON: THE SHOPPING CART

Ever since its launch in July 1995, Amazon.com has epitomized e-commerce. The shopping cart model pioneered by the original online bookseller is now ubiquitous for the purchase of standardized products. Let's break it down with you in the user's shoes.

1. You go to the site and search for a product or browse through one of the product categories.

2. You select an individual product from a list or a large grid of thumbnail images. This brings you to a page where a single product is displayed.

3. This product information page has everything you might want to know about the product—including photographs, pricing, product specs, user reviews, and ratings.

4. After reading one or more product information pages, you make a selection and add the item to your shopping cart.

5. You now either continue shopping or proceed through the checkout process.

The strategy for shopping cart sites is simple: give the user a broad selection and ample information to help him find the right product. Then all roads should lead to the product page and the big "buy" button. From there, it's okay to throw in a little cross-selling, but it's important not to distract the user from reaching his and your goal line: the checkout counter.

Walmart.com, JCrew.com, and any number of other retail sites all work this way. Across the Web, this is by far the most popular e-commerce model. It's also what users understand and expect to see—they know the paradigm, so no matter where on the Web they land, they find the shopping cart simple, easy to use, reliable, and trustworthy. It's wholly usable.

The advantage of this experience is that it works; the problem is that it threatens to commoditize the retail experience. Visit any site with a shopping cart and you'll find a similar layout on the product page. Cover up the logos and color schemes and the casual user would be hard pressed to tell one brand from another. Commoditization of the retail experience extends to the commoditization of products. With category pages consisting of rows of thumbnail images of nearly identical-looking products, and product pages with a small image in the top-left corner of the page surrounded by product stats, from a user perspective the products themselves start blending together—a scary prospect for any manufacturer dependent on online sales.

To fight commoditization, companies look for the experience to differentiate. This is where adding fun, such as social shopping or compelling content such as videos and articles (see the higher calling and bilateral customer-service chapters for more ideas), and conveniences, such as saved shopping lists and credit card information, is important to break down the monotony and make the experience more memorable.

MODEL #2 ZIPCAR: THE CONVERSION FUNNEL

Zipcar is not your average car rental company. You can pick from cars such as Mini Coopers or hybrids; filling up the tank is free; and users sign up with annual or monthly memberships.

To sell its membership plans, Zipcar uses what I call the conversion funnel model of site design. The concept is simple: Zipcar sells one thing, so the entire site is just a funnel guiding the users toward the purchase. Here's how it works.

When you visit Zipcar for the first time as a prospective customer, you land on a simple home page. On the left is a carousel of photos showing people enjoying the use of a car to shop, go kayaking, and head to a business meeting. On the right are three large buttons. One is to join, one shows its forty-five thousand "likes" on Facebook, and the other communicates Zipcar's value proposition in five short sentences. On the bottom is a large banner touting the simplicity of signing up. "Learn about the 4 simple steps to Zipcar freedom: 1. Join, 2. Reserve, 3. Unlock, 4. Drive," it reads. The top of the page lets potential users select their city or university and get more information about the program—"rates & plans," "find cars," "how it works," "is Zipcar for me?," and "join!" The only areas of added complexity are the tabs for corporate and university memberships and the fine print at the far bottom.

It's easy to move ahead—just click on one of the prominent join buttons, and you're led to a simple and clean page that reads, "Let's get you started. Joining is as easy as pie. Mmmmm, pie." Then you select the type of membership: individual, business, or university. Directly after choosing to join as an individual, you're prompted to choose a user name and password for a new account. With this, the user can stop and start the application process as needed because the system saves his progress. Then as users continue through the funnel, Zipcar's phone number is prominently presented in case they want any live help.

Everything in this experience is designed toward one end—giving the user a clear path to complete the transaction. The site is small and simple: it quickly communicates what the product is, states a clear value proposition, and then presents a big button to buy. All other pages on the site exist only to answer basic, need-to-know questions that ultimately encourage the user to make the purchase. From a management standpoint, these sites are primed for analytics—it's easy to constantly test new offers, marketing messages, and refinements to the conversion funnel to maximize sales.

This model works for companies that sell limited products or services—you'll note there is no shopping cart; the entire site is just a big checkout flow. This kind of site works well for subscription-oriented services such as buying cell phone service; and it works well for one-time purchases that require a lot of configuration, like ordering an airline ticket or pizza. For these kinds of goods, often a shopping cart doesn't make sense. Either there aren't enough products to put in a cart or the item needs to be customized beyond what a typical product-information page can do. So the site is essentially a big step-by-step form coupled with a clear value proposition, which is very user-friendly; it just explains why people should buy and then it gets out of the way so they can purchase.

Often, once a user becomes a customer, conversion funnel sites shift to a tailored application to help the user manage his or her purchase. In other words, once you subscribe to Zipcar, you then log in to manage your account and reserve cars; after you buy a ticket at Delta.com you can manage your flights; after signing up with a mobile-service provider, you can go online to check your usage, upgrade your plan, and monitor your monthly bills.

The typical mistake companies make with the conversion funnel is to overcomplicate the public site. Too much detailed, unnecessary information about the company and products just creates confusion for users. Everything in the funnel should be designed with one question in mind: is this information that a user needs to know to make the purchase? If not, it doesn't belong.

MODEL #3 ANGRY BIRDS: FREEMIUM MODEL

It's a fact: you or someone you know likes to play Angry Birds. It's a wildly popular game where players use a slingshot to lob colorful birds at structures protecting evil green pigs. Besides being addictive, it's also an example of an increasingly popular e-commerce model, the freemium approach to sales. In this model, users are given a free, often ad-supported, limited version of a digital product or service. The company then makes money by enticing existing users with upsells meant to enhance the experience.

When Angry Birds debuted in December 2009, its Finnish developer, Rovio Mobile, offered two versions in the Apple App Store. The "lite" version was free and included a limited number of levels. The complete "paid" version costs ninety-nine cents. A year later the free version had been downloaded thirty million times, and the paid version had been downloaded twelve million times. In December 2010, Rovio introduced a ninety-nine-cent upsell: the "Mighty Eagle" character. If players purchased this, they could use it to unlock difficult levels and advance in the game, thereby providing an incentive to keep on playing.

Like the conversion funnel, the freemium model is often used by companies that sell single products and services. But while the goal of the conversion funnel is to get payment upfront, freemium seeks to entice buyers with free samples. It tends to work best with digital products, because it seizes on the opportunity to continually sell immediately accessible updates and enhancements at nominal charges.

While game companies pioneered the model, today it's used to sell all types of digital services. Dropbox, the online file storage and sharing system, gives users two gigabytes of storage for free and then charges for more. Pandora, the streaming music service, offers every visitor forty hours of free, ad-supported listening per month. Users who want an ad-free experience or unlimited listening privileges can pay a relatively small fee. LinkedIn, the business social networking site, provides all users a free basic version, but has tiered upgrades that offer progressively deeper levels of information useful for effective networking. Skype offers free computer-to-computer calling, but charges for calls to cell phones and a premium service with more features.

In all of these cases, the company's goal is to give users something of value for free, and then to convert a certain percentage into paying customers. Free users can often be considered a marketing cost. The more users there are on LinkedIn, the more valuable it is for someone to pay for improved access to the network. Even though Dropbox has to pay the storage costs for people who use the service for free, those people are also likely to tell their friends about Dropbox and some of them will likely sign up for the premium service.

MODEL #4 ZILLOW: HUMAN-ASSISTED SALES

There are some products and services users can research extensively on the Web and get very close to purchasing, but people are needed to conduct the final transaction. Sites that sell these kinds of major products and services are designed to lead users as far as possible through an automated and convenient shopping process with live interaction only necessary to facilitate the final deal and validate the transaction. (Note: These types of services tend to be better for users who have a do-it-yourself mentality. We'll learn more about them in the next chapter.)

The real-estate industry is increasingly heading this way, sped along by sites including Zillow and Redfin. On Zillow, which launched in 2006, someone shopping for a home can find block-by-block information about homes for sale; total square footage; number of bedrooms and bathrooms; compare one home against another; and even get price estimates on properties that aren't on the market. In the past, the person would have had to rely on a real-estate agent for this information. Now it can all be done before ever coming face-to-face with a human being. Zillow labels itself a "media" business. It gets its revenues from advertising, mostly ads by real estate agents. This essentially makes Zillow and agents partners: Zillow provides research tools, and agents, linked to on the page, close the deals.

Redfin.com has taken this model a step further, actively seeking to eliminate the middleman. Like Zillow, Redfin offers a ton of information about homes for sale including pricing history, photos of the interior and exterior, the year built, square footage, lot size, and other important details. But Redfin actually employs real estate agents. So when a buyer sees a home she's interested in, she can schedule an in-person viewing online with one of its agents or immediately send the service an offer for the home. Because the buyer is doing so much of the research and discovery work by herself, Redfin agents spend most of their time completing negotiations and paperwork. As a result, Redfin usually rebates about half of its commission from the sellers to the homebuyers—a win for the user!

In this middle ground between fully automated and fully human sales, the key to success is providing clear and comprehensive information about the products and the buying process, and then standardizing the human interaction element. Redfin, for example, offers a great deal of how-to information on its site, but it also educates users with regularly scheduled local-area home buying classes and it provides an "offer wizard" to help buyers make their own offers. When an agent gets involved, his or her role is limited to showing homes and preparing the transactional documents. With this model, Redfin has been able to realize all of the efficiency and scale possible from e-commerce for a transaction that ten years ago required intensive and expensive person-to-person communications.

MODEL #5 GOLDMAN SACHS: DRIVE-TO-PHONE

Admittedly there are the businesses where the sales process hasn't gone digital and probably never will. Some buying decisions are just too dependent on personalization and interaction with human beings. For example, if you were looking to hire an architect to design a house, you'd no doubt want to sit down and discuss your ideas. In this case, human interaction is an integral part of choosing the right service provider. But this doesn't mean architects can ignore digital media. They still must have a strong online presence. Most users will begin their search for the service provider online, examining several Web sites of local architects, reading about their qualifications, and examining the projects they've completed. For businesses like this, the Web site is often the first point of contact with them—and if it's inadequate or nonexistent, prospective customers won't even get to the point of saying hello.

To be most effective for the user and the business, the site must readily showcase the company's credibility, qualifications, experience, and track record—it should almost be like a glorified brochure. Once this essential need-to-know information is provided, the site should be designed to actively encourage users to contact the company by e-mail, online form, or phone—after all, that's their next logical step and it's the only way a sale will be made. The savviest companies in this space use analytics to track what brings people to their sites, the information they look at, and the pages that lead them to make initial contact. This allows the company to optimize the user experience and measure their site's efficiency through statistics such as cost-per-acquisition.

A more advanced approach for companies offering professional services is to establish thought leadership in their industry areas. That means displaying their expertise by publishing white papers, advice, and information that will be useful to prospective clients. This boosts credibility and serves as outbound utility marketing, driving in more leads. One example is the Web site of Goldman Sachs, the investment bank. Its site contains an ideas section that houses articles, videos, and publications about different subject areas related to the economy, investing, and business. Content like this can help generate incremental traffic and awareness through search and socializing—people can find this content on Google, and the content can be discussed and commented upon in blogs and discussion groups around the Web. But in the end, this information does not complete a sale. A salesperson is needed to close the deal.

MATCHING THE FIVE MODELS AND TCPF

The five online shopping models and TCPF hold the keys for a user-driven selling experience for your business. The first step is to clearly understand which of the five models is a fit for your business; then you couple this with a decision about which areas—trust, convenience, price, or fun—you'll focus on to win. Finally, it's about your digital core executing a great experience that brings it all to life. In combination, any company can have a solid plan to convert users to customers in a way that ensures high levels of user satisfaction.

But what happens after the user decides to buy? What should a user-first business do to keep customers happy and encourage return purchases? It all comes down to bilateral customer service, discussed next.

CHAPTER SUMMARY: TCPF SALES

Market Insights

- People make purchases from the channel that wins on trust, convenience, price, and fun (TCPF). Over time, e-commerce sites have become more convenient, price-competitive, trustworthy, and fun for an increasingly wide range of products and services.

- Users shop online in very predictable ways, based on the kind of product or service under consideration. Five proven e-commerce models are *shopping cart, conversion funnel, freemium, human-assisted sales,* and *drive-to-phone.*

Strategic Imperatives

- User-first companies should have an e-commerce strategy, regardless of product or service category, and this strategy should be oriented toward the TCPF proclivities of their users.

- The traditional barrier to selling online is uncertainty: the product or service is too difficult to explain; the prospective buyer needs to hold, touch, or interact with it; or, pricing is uncertain. Effective user-first companies must find a way around these barriers to enable digital transactions with their users. Critical to this is standardization of product offering and transparency in pricing.

- Companies should embrace one of the five online sales models that's most appropriate to their business, as defined above. Once the standard model is implemented, the organization can then ramp up the TCPF levers to match their users' preferences.

- With convenience a primary driver of sales, the companies that can extend their footprint to as many convenient locations—through mobile, APIs, and integration with a physical presence—are the ones that are best set to achieve great overall sales growth. It's why companies experiment with same-day delivery, order online/pickup in store, and other models of commerce. They want to meet the needs of as many users as possible.

7

Bilateral Customer Service

Combine Self-Service and Full-Service to Keep People Coming Back for More

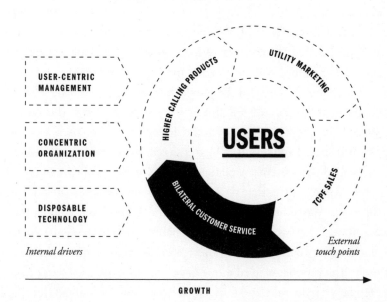

About a year ago, when my second son was born, my wife and I decided it was time to move to a larger apartment. The new place came equipped with an apartment-wide stereo system. There were speakers in every room, which were hooked up to one central system with a big player that could store fifty CDs—fifty CDs! Too bad I don't own any CDs. So it was time to buy a new stereo system—digital, of course, with the ultimate goal of playing MP3s in one room, Pandora in a second, and NPR in the third. Not knowing where to start, I Googled the brand name of this marvel of entertainment technology, circa 1995, that was included in the price of my apartment. A few clicks later I ended up on Crutchfield.com, a home electronics retailer.

As soon as I landed on the home page, I found a tab for "support" and another one for "forums." The Web site had tons of helpful articles and videos about home stereo systems, including details on different kinds of equipment, how they compared, and how to hook them up. The articles were all written by a real person who worked at Crutchfield— Amanda, the audiovisual editor, whose bio was there for me to read. Within minutes, I had done enough research to realize that what I really needed was to talk to a live person. At the top of every page was a phone number where I could reach "expert advisers" seven days a week; I was even told that three representatives were available right now, waiting for my call. So I dialed the number. Within seconds, I had an "expert" on the phone. I explained to him how my apartment was laid out and what I had in each room. While on the phone, he had me unscrew the control panel on the wall so I could tell him how it was connected to the wiring. He then asked me what kind of audio I wanted to use, such as CDs, DVDs, Web-based audio sites, TV, and so on. Then based on all that, he recommended two systems, explained the pros and cons of each one, and even helped me whittle that down to one option, which he helped me purchase over the phone, after waiting for me to check out competitors' prices online. (They were so helpful I probably would have spent an extra few bucks to buy with them, but their prices were the same as the competition.) The product arrived a few days later with a signed letter from the company's namesake and CEO with his personal e-mail address.

Crutchfield hits all the right customer-service notes for our digital age. The company's Web site supports "self-service" with massive amounts of customer support in various formats: forums, videos, articles—you name it, the site has it. But it also provides easy access to live, well-trained customer-service representatives. The salesperson I spoke with was not only responsive to my individual needs but well informed about the company's products and their capabilities. All the information I could ever want was up front and available, including pricing deals and shipping fees. My order arrived quickly, and when I returned a small component of the system, the process was hassle free. The company's motto? "We're all about making good connections."

Founded by its namesake CEO Bill Crutchfield in 1974, the company started as a mail-order business selling car stereos to do-it-yourselfers. But business got off to a slow start. "Sales our first year were terrible," the company story goes. So Crutchfield went to the source to figure out what was going awry. He mailed out a questionnaire to a few hundred of his customers asking them what they thought was wrong with the catalogue and the business overall. What he found out was that most of them were intimidated by the thought of installing a car stereo. As a solution, Crutchfield decided to fill the catalogue with all kinds of information to help his customers overcome their intimidation. Today, the company, five hundred employees strong, has expertly maintained its commitment to customer service. With ample tools and information for DIY customers and a high-quality approach to old-school, person-to-person customer service, Crutchfield has adapted beautifully to our digital age.

And that's no small feat. Digital technologies have made customer service much more complicated than it used to be—it's no longer about training employees in basic customer-service techniques and then keeping them motivated. The Web has opened up channels of communication that didn't exist in the mainstream two decades ago, such as e-mail, FAQs, live chat, support forums, Twitter, and Facebook. As a result, customer expectations about company responsiveness and transparency have exploded. They want to be able to make a purchase online with as little interference as possible—but then once they decide they need personal help, they want the same warm and helpful touch they could get from the mom-and-pop stores of old. User-first companies understand that the best way to guarantee customer satisfaction is to meet these two seemingly contradictory needs of today's online users: self-service and full-service.

SELF-SERVICE VS. FULL-SERVICE

In 2007, Stanley Fish, a humanities professor and frequent contributor to *The New York Times* opinion pages, sparked a debate over what today's customers want when he wrote a column criticizing an unnamed coffee chain that sounded a lot like Starbucks. Once, he wrote, you simply went into a diner, ordered a coffee and a cheese Danish from a waitress, and had it set before you in a matter of seconds. Now, he complained in a tone reminiscent of an old *Seinfeld* episode, "you have to get in line, and you may have one or two people in front of you who are ordering a drink with more parts than an internal combustion engine, something about 'double shot,' 'skinny,' 'breve,' 'grande,' 'au lait,' and a lot of other words that never pass my lips."

After you get your coffee, the real confusion starts, Fish complained: "There is a staggering array of [accessories], and the order of their placement seems random in relation to the order of your needs . . . After all, there are so many items to reach for—lids, cup jackets, straws, napkins, stirrers, milk, half-and-half, water, sugar, Splenda, the wastepaper basket, spoons."

Fish had a point. In our Starbucks world, we've lost the simplicity of ordering a coffee and having someone fix it for us. Of course, we gain the advantage of choice—adding the type of milk and sweetener we prefer in the amounts we want. This is much the same change that's been ushered in by the Internet: we've traded the simplicity of walking into the local electronics store and asking a salesperson for the best stereo to meet our needs for going online to access more choice, more information, more control over the product we purchase—even if that means we have to do a little more work. But at the same time, consumer electronics stores such as Crutchfield and Best Buy still value the role of the friendly, well-informed salesperson for those of us who prefer the straightforwardness of interacting with a human being. The smartest companies maintain a traditional, personable approach to customer service in addition to ample, less costly self-service options for the sizeable number of people who may want to have a real person walk them through a transaction.

The 318 comments posted below Fish's article were nearly evenly split between readers who sympathized with him and others who found him to be "a cranky old man." One hit on precisely the issue of what many customers expect from companies in the digital era. He positioned himself as someone "*very* happy" to have the opportunity to put his own milk in his coffee. "It gives me the control that I want," he says. He then went on to reference a trip to a Dunkin' Donuts in West Virginia where it took the counter person three times to understand he didn't want sugar in his joe.

"It's a different world now, Mr. Fish, and it's about having things the way we want it, not the way the person behind the counter wants it," he sharply continued. "You might have been able to get a cheese Danish and a cup of brewed coffee in twenty seconds years ago and there are still places you can do that. However I am glad that today there are places for people like me who prefer things like a triple grande skim latte and a whole wheat muffin."

The trick for any company looking to excel in the digital media environment is that it must accommodate both types of customers at the same time—Stanley Fish and Mr. Triple Grande Skim Latte. I call this approach bilateral customer service.

THE DIGITAL DO-IT-YOURSELFERS

Today's users, and especially post-digitals (discussed in the introductory chapter), often want to know everything, understand everything, and do everything online without having to wait and interact with a person. Interaction with a human being is often viewed as annoying, frustrating, and slow. For them, good customer service is self-service. Companies that understand this consumer mindset ensure that every possible interaction between the firm and customer can be done online. Product information, product comparisons, reviews, and competitive pricing information are all clearly available. You shouldn't even have to go to a store to see the product. In the ideal scenario, the item will just get shipped to you, for free, with free returns.

Amazon's Web Services offering, which sells cloud-computing services, is a great example of customer service geared toward the digital do-it-yourselfer. All of its more than twenty services are available online on demand. Users sign up, enter their credit card information, and get immediate access to pay-as-you-go cloud storage space, bulk e-mail sending tools, Amazon's fulfillment capabilities, an on-demand global workforce for "human intelligence tasks," and many more services. Other companies that offer similar types of products often require expensive setup costs, interaction with a salesperson, and high levels of technical expertise. Amazon Web Services eliminates all those hurdles by allowing full account creation and management online, all human-free.

Most of the time, Internet users are like Starbucks drinkers: they have a do-it-yourself mentality. They want to be in control and they want to do everything themselves. But the only way this works is if the information and the tools are readily available. The worst possible customer-service scenario is when a user can't find what she's looking for or can't do what she planned on doing, so she is forced by poor usability to hunt for a customer-service phone number, punch in that number, listen to a recorded message, follow a series of prompts, and sit on hold to finally speak to a live person who may or may not be prepared to address the user's need. For the company, putting a user through these steps is a categorical failure. But this isn't an uncommon once-in-a-blue-moon chain of events. It's all too easy, almost natural, for company employees who live and breathe the products every day to forget the degree to which customers do not understand their products and services (think of Crutchfield and his car stereos circa 1974). Company sites need to be both comprehensive and carefully organized so users can find what they need.

What does self-service look like when it's done right? Some examples:

- **Frequently asked questions:** Considering that many users visit company Web sites in order to answer questions they have, Digital Leadership Set companies often anticipate user queries and then design their Web sites and FAQ (frequently asked questions) pages in order to address them.

  If you visit the Web site of Walt Disney World, for example, you'll find that it's designed to answer many questions that a potential visitor to one of its parks or resorts might have. As soon as the page loads, a user's eye is drawn to a navigation bar on the top that includes buttons for "Parks," "Places to Stay," "Things to Do," "Where to Eat," and "Tickets and Packages." Hovering over any of these brings up a list of more specific options including such valuable user information as "Guests with Disabilities," "Spas," and "Discounts for Florida Residents." If this isn't enough, further links lead to more in-depth information. A user can quickly work her way around the Web site to find out whatever she needs to know about a potential vacation to the park. It's set up as an intuitive FAQ page, guiding the user through the experience and answering her questions at every step. But for those users who want to find out answers to specific questions without the larger discovery process, there is a thorough FAQ page with multiple questions and answers about dining, the Disney Rewards Visa card, hurricane policy, smoke-free policy, passport and visa information, and much more. All of this self-service information, however, doesn't mean Disney is dissuading people to call. On the right side of the FAQ page are nine distinct customer-service phone numbers.

The FAQ paradigm can be done in ways that don't even look like a conventional FAQ—but are still designed to meet core user needs. When NYC & Company—the city of New York's official marketing, tourism, and partnership organization—redesigned its site, NYCGO.com, in 2008, the organization realized that one of the most common questions for people visiting New York is: "What should I do?" Everyone knows the top tourist sites of the city, such as the Statue of Liberty and the Empire State Building. What people really want to know about are the things locals do that they can't read about in guidebooks. So New York City & Co. solicited advice from locals, both ordinary and famous, to build a page called "Just Ask the Locals." It features Blondie front-woman Debbie Harry's five favorite spots to see live music, *Top Chef* host Padma Lakshmi dishing on her preferred spice stores, and fashion expert Tim Gunn's top venues for fashion bargains. As a result, the site makes it easy for people to plan a unique and memorable trip to the city.

- **Support forums and bulletin boards:** Users can be extremely good at answering each other's questions. If you have a problem with a Hewlett-Packard computer or printer, you can visit its online support forum for help. The forum hosts hundreds of user-to-user discussions on issues ranging from how to receive a fax to upgrading to Windows 7 to adding a graphics card for a better gaming experience. HP experts monitor the discussions and offer answers to questions, but the majority of solutions spring from the very active community of participants. To encourage the conversation, in the "Best of the Community" section, HP administrators highlight especially useful user tips every week. In addition to this DIY trove of information, HP maintains a section of its Web site that makes it easy for users to find and download drivers for its printers, which is especially useful for anyone who wants to use a printer with a new computer, or use a new printer with an old computer. HP's online repository empowers users to solve many common computer and printer problems on their own, reducing the reasons they'd have to pick up the phone and wait on hold for a representative.

- **Knowledge centers:** Microsoft sells some of the most complicated products in the world—software systems to large corporations. It addresses its complex customer-service needs through MSDN, the Microsoft developer's network, an online resource of helpful documentation, example code, discussions boards, and other tools to help developers solve their technical problems as they relate to Microsoft software. This comprehensive level of information is an effective solution for companies that don't want to frustrate DIY customers or rake up hours and hours of call center time—it's about bringing unrivaled transparency to the business. This kind of documentation should be so comprehensive that the firm's own customer-service representatives can use it to solve customer problems when they do pick up the phone.

THE FULL-SERVICE USER

The other side of customer service in the digital era is that sometimes users want the luxury of someone else adding the milk and sugar to their coffee. This full-service offering can take many forms. The smartest companies use it in a way that makes the organization feel transparent, accessible, and helpful.

What does this look like? Try visiting the Apple store in New York City's SoHo neighborhood on a Saturday morning. On the ground floor, customers buzz around maple tables displaying the latest Apple products, using MacBook computers to check their e-mail and log on to Facebook. Soft light streams in through a skylight that runs the length of the ceiling. Blue-shirted Apple employees mingle with the crowd ready to answer questions if asked, but otherwise stay out of the way.

On the second floor, at the top of a set of translucent stairs lit from below, customers are seated auditorium style listening to a bearded Apple employee teach them about how to get the most from the Mac OS X operating system.

Nearby, the fifty-foot "Genius Bar" runs along one wall. Customers sit on black stools while Apple "geniuses" hunch over to inspect their laptops and iPods. At two tables set up at the end of the bar, more Apple employees give one-to-one tutorials, showing new customers how to use their computers. These aren't just any old people hired off the street and deposited onto the showroom floor either—each Apple genius gets two weeks of training at the headquarters in Cupertino. Except in the case where more intensive repair services are needed, their services are free.

Apple, of course, has support pages on the Internet for all its products. If you have a problem with your iPod, for example, the answer is likely to be there. But if you want to see a real person, all you have to do is fill out an online form to make a reservation at the nearest Genius Bar.

The message to the customer is clear: if you buy an Apple product, your customer-service options are limitless—a valuable quality of companies in the Digital Leadership Set.

From a branding standpoint, the real win to full-service is that the organization starts to be perceived less as a faceless, anonymous machine and more as a group of people who really care and want to make their customers happy. This kind of service forms an emotional connection between customer and company that can last a lifetime.

Of course, few companies have retail spaces in high-traffic locations across the world, or the resources to meet to the full-service needs of their customers. But leading digital companies do find ways to put a human face on their customer service operations. Here are a few different approaches:

- **Multichannel.** Some companies provide multiple avenues for customer contact. Digital Leadership Set member Best Buy excels at this. For example, if a customer wants face-to-face contact, he can visit one of the Geek Squad desks located inside any Best Buy store, or can even arrange a house call. Best Buy also rigorously maintains its Facebook page, and in addition, the company has its "Twelpforce," which includes thousands of Best Buy employees—not just customer-service reps—who have signed up to respond to customer questions via Twitter. Barry Judge, Best Buy's chief marketing officer, says the idea behind Twelpforce is to "make it as easy as possible for people to complain." A customer who wants to contact Best Buy has no shortage of options.

- **Phone number prominence.** A lot of companies see customer service as an expense that drags down the bottom line. They see the Internet as a way to reduce staffing costs, so they replace real people with a list of FAQs on their site. They then outsource their call centers and bury the contact number on their Web site in a tiny font to discourage users from calling. But there are plenty of occasions, even with the most comprehensive FAQ, when users need and/or want to talk to a real, live person. One way that leading digital companies differentiate themselves is by posting their 1-800 numbers right up front on their Web sites, as in the case of Crutchfield.com. This sends customers the message that they should feel free to call if they need to. Zappos is another example of companies that have also taken this route. "We view any expense that enhances the customer experience as a marketing cost because it generates more repeat customers through word of mouth," says Zappos CEO Tony Hsieh.

- **Constant stream of new self-service communications.** Another way to keep in contact with your customers is to have employees maintain company blogs and/or Twitter streams. Google uses these communications to keep their users in the loop and connected to product developments. For the curious, Google maintains dozens of blogs and corresponding Twitter streams. You can read tips and updates about Google products such as Google Maps, Gmail, and YouTube; keep up with Google-related developments in countries from South Korea to Hungary; find information about working with products such as the Android operating system; learn how to get the most out of Google advertising services; keep up with Google's latest research initiatives; and follow its position on public policy. This constant stream of information helps to humanize the company and aids transparency. It gives a sense that the end user is directly involved in the product, which helps build trust between the brand and its users.

WHAT GOOGLE DIDN'T DO

As an Internet-based company from the get-go, Google was able to get away with not having any physical retail centers or live customer support—until early 2010, that is. In January, to great excitement from Google fans and attention from the media, the Internet giant began selling its first-ever piece of hardware, the Nexus One touch screen smart phone, solely through its own Web store. Its goal was to revolutionize the cell phone buying market, allowing users to buy devices without having to go through their carriers. But the company—perhaps used to providing online support for its free services—underestimated users' full-service expectations. When the phone hit the market, Google had only set up some online FAQs, customer support forums, and an e-mail service that said it could take forty-eight hours to respond to. There was no way to reach a Google customer-service representative by phone.

When the phone landed in customer mailboxes, many of the new owners had problems getting its 3G connectivity to work. And those who tried to reach Google were stymied. So they called T-Mobile and HTC, which had manufactured the phone under contract, but those companies generally directed people to back to Google. This only frustrated users more. Many resorted to filling Google's public online forums with enraged comments such as this one: "Dear Google, I used to love you, now I hate you. Keep your stupid phone." Within days of the phone's release, the media picked up on the fiasco. *Wired* published the headline "Google Nexus One Leaves Customers Sour." *The New York Times* wrote, "Hey Google, Anybody Home?" *USA TODAY* went with the headline "Google's Nexus One Phone Sparks Flood of Complaints."

The following month, a chastened Google began to offer phone support. However, the damage was already done. After about five months, Google announced the closing of its Web store; after seven months on the market, Google discontinued the Nexus One due to poor sales. Google had failed to provide adequate full-service customer support, and this helped cause the failure of its grand ambition.

THE POWER OF THE DIGITAL SWARM

In October 2009, a Yelp user named Sean C. gave a two-star review to Ocean Avenue Books, a San Francisco used bookstore. "This place is a *total mess* with minimal organization of titles or subjects," Sean C. wrote. "I think this place needs to close down for a few days and do a thorough cleaning and organization and get rid of all the crap!"

As far as Yelp reviews go, it was far from the most scathing, and might even have been good advice. The store's owner, however, didn't appreciate it. Within a few hours, she began to barrage Sean C. with a series of offensive e-mails sent through Yelp, accusing him of being "stupid looking," "a coward," and from a "bad family," in addition to casting aspersions on his mother. "You are low class—you look it. You look like trash," she wrote.

Two days after the review was posted, the bookstore owner showed up at Sean C.'s apartment—it's unclear how she found it, since the Yelp review was supposed to be anonymous—and tried to force her way in. According to Sean C. in another Yelp posting, "After a serious struggle I was able to repel her back outside and get the door locked and call 911." The police came and took the bookstore owner in for psychiatric observation.

This, of course, was not a productive way to respond to a negative review. But it demonstrates the power and influence of one single dissatisfied customer. Gone are the days when an unhappy patron would tell a few friends about his bad experience, who might in turn tell a few more friends (just like Heather Locklear in the classic 1980s Faberge TV commercial—Google it) . . . and that's about it. Now it's possible for an unhappy camper to scale up the bad publicity exponentially by posting negative comments on a company Web site, blogging about a bad experience, sending out an angry tweet to followers, creating a Web site about how much the company "sucks," or even posting a Facebook status update to his nine hundred–plus friends lambasting a retailer for bad customer service. Every customer is a user, and as was noted in chapter 5, these user reviews carry a lot of weight in online communities. And this chatter about your company is searchable on the Web 24/7, available to any potential new customers. The Internet doesn't forget anything. Every customer comment is there forever for users to see.

THE DIGITAL MEA CULPA

The reality of customer service is that no company is perfect. If customers demanded a perfect experience each time they interacted with an organization, all companies would be out of business. In our research, we consistently find that users *will* tolerate product and service problems—provided their complaints are quickly addressed by real people at the company who are transparent about the issue, are responsive, and show that they really care.

On January 21, 2010, Toyota—a company that had built its reputation on the quality of its cars—announced a recall of more than two million vehicles due to what the company labeled a problem with the accelerator. The recall was greeted with a flood of news reports linking the malfunction to nineteen deaths. To compound this bad situation, in early February, Toyota had to announce another recall, this time of its popular Prius models, to fix a reported problem with the braking system.

Toyota's initial response to these recalls and the deluge of damaging news media attention was a case study of how not to handle a public relations crisis, and by extension a customer-service crisis. At first the company tried to avoid the problems. Company president Akio Toyoda, the grandson of the founder, simply disappeared from view for the first two weeks. This didn't do any good. During those key fourteen days, the company's share price slid 17 percent. With the brand's reputation in seeming free fall, Jim Lentz, the chief operating officer of Toyota Motor Sales, USA, stood up to try to stanch the bleeding himself. He appeared on the *Today* show to explain to Matt Lauer Toyota's response to the critical situation.

Lentz complemented his traditional media-relations efforts by reaching out to Toyota's digital community—which was also in an uproar. On February 1, Lentz posted an effusive video apology on YouTube, announcing that Toyota was going to keep many of its dealerships open for extended hours in order to fix the problems with its cars. "I apologize for this situation and I hope you'll give us a chance to earn back your trust," Lentz said. Later that day, Lentz took questions from Toyota users over Twitter.

Toyota also set up a video Q&A to be broadcast on Digg, a social news Web site, inviting the site's users to send in questions for Lentz, who would answer the ten most popular as determined by user votes. Doug Frisbie, a social media manager for Toyota Motor Sales, told *AdWeek,*

"[The appearance on Digg] allowed us to take a much more conversational approach, which for a big brand is difficult to do. Social media allows brands to become more humanized."

In the three days before the interview, Digg users submitted fourteen hundred questions. Surprisingly, in spite of the loud, attention-grabbing digital ire spewing at the company, Toyota's users didn't have questions about the recalls. Only four of the top ten were about the crisis. Some people had questions about car design, others about vehicles that would run without gas. The most popular question, with 289 votes, was a personal one for Lentz: "What do you drive?" In its first five days online, the Lentz interview racked up over one million views.

The company's sales—aided by generous discount offers—sprang back the following month. Sales for March 2010 came in at 41 percent above the same month the year prior. It's hard to quantify how much Toyota's social media responses contributed to this rebound, but if anything, the sales rise and the softball questions posed by Digg users showed the disconnect between the concerns of the public and the focus of the media. Lentz's adoption of digital tools allowed him to bypass reporters and communicate directly with Toyota's user base.

Whenever a company faces a major outcry from consumers, a quick, transparent, and authentic response is of critical importance. This is what Groupon CEO Andrew Mason did in early 2011.

In January, five hundred Japanese Groupon users put money down to take advantage of a deal for a New Year's Eve food delivery from Bird Cafe. But it was too many customers for the restaurant to handle, and this resulted in late deliveries and food that arrived in poor condition. Customers directly affected by the flub were reimbursed, sent an apology, and offered vouchers worth up to five thousand yen (about sixty dollars). But still after this peace offering, Mason released a frank, genuine, and seemingly script-free video apology on YouTube, admitting his company "really messed up." Mason used his public address (delivered in English with Japanese subtitles) to shed light on the behind-the-scenes human error that led to the problem, thereby helping to restore customer trust. "We've encountered this type of problem before," Mason admitted. He explained that in the United States, where Groupon had already been operating for two years, the company had developed capacity planning formulas to help businesses identify the level of customer demand they could support. But Groupon hadn't rolled out those capacity plans in Japan yet. "Popularity of Groupon Japan has grown so quickly it took us off guard and we weren't expecting to run into this problem so quickly," he confessed. He promised users that they had immediately started training staff in Japan and that from now on, as the company expanded to new markets, they would only launch with those capacity formulas in place.

With their public mea culpas, both Mason and Lentz were following in the digital footsteps of JetBlue founder and CEO David Neeleman. He is famous for posting a video of a sincere apology on YouTube following an incident in 2007 where the now Digital Leadership Set company's passengers were left stranded on the tarmac in New York for eleven hours following a winter snowstorm. His apology and subsequent creation of a "Customer Bill of Rights" have since become industry best practice.

THE DIGITAL SUGGESTION BOX

But companies cannot just take a crisis-management approach to customer service, doing nothing until there is a big blow-up involving customers and users, and then saying sorry. The best way to harness the energy of the digital swarm and redirect it in your company's favor is to invite users to communicate with your company directly. Comcast, for example, in response to its customer-service issues, established a Twitter feed, @ComcastCares, which provides transparent customer service from helpful, real people who work at Comcast. The result was a burst of positive publicity about Comcast's efforts to improve its customer service, and scores of new happy customers.

Other companies are also starting to experiment with ways for users to make suggestions directly through their own Web sites. This helps reduce the need for users to turn to alternatives like Yelp, creates a feeling that the company cares about its users' opinions, and involves users in helping the team come up with ideas to improve the business. Dell tried this approach with its IdeaStorm initiative to great initial success.

Dell knows what it's like to be pummeled online—and not just by your average user. On June 21, 2005, the popular blogger Jeff Jarvis, author of *What Would Google Do?*, published a post on his BuzzMachine blog where he wrote that he'd just bought a new Dell computer with a four-year warrant that included in-home service. The computer was a "lemon," Jarvis wrote, but the company was refusing to come to his house to fix it.

It could have been a one-off rant from a frustrated customer, except that Jarvis (who as of May 2011 has more than sixty-six thousand Twitter followers) wasn't an average user. He was an influencer, and with his rant came dozens of other disappointed Dell customers posting comments on his blog about their problems with the company. This outpouring resulted in a series on the blog called "Dell Hell." Other blogs, newspapers, and magazines then picked up the content. After nearly ten days of frustration with Dell's customer service, Jarvis reported that he'd gone out and bought a Mac.

All of the attention reinforced a perception that the company made shoddy products and did not care about its customers. Recognizing this problem, in 2006, Dell began a concerted response to engage its customers online and avoid a Dell Hell repeat. One step was to contact bloggers who criticized the company in order to address their complaints directly. It also launched Direct2Dell, a site where Dell representatives blogged about the company's products and other technology news in a credible, personable voice. These efforts are admirable and those that a Digital Leadership Set company should undertake.

Then, in February 2007, Dell took a great stride forward, launching IdeaStorm, a Web site dedicated to soliciting ideas from Dell users—essentially a community forum where people post ideas about how to improve Dell's products. Site users vote for or against the ideas, so that popular ones move to the top. In the meantime, company employees acknowledge receipt of each idea and indicate whether it is being taken into consideration. According to Dell, there have been more than ten thousand ideas posted on the site, of which nearly four hundred have been adopted—major ones include offering the Linux operating system on new Dell computers and offering buyers of particular products the option to opt out of the promotional "bloatware" installed on their new computers.

Starbucks faced a similar quality and service issue in 2007 and 2008, and this, combined with a poor economy, pushed Starbucks sales into a downward tailspin. Founder Howard Schultz returned to the CEO position, and shortly thereafter the company launched MyStarbucksIdea. At the time, Schultz acknowledged that rapid expansion had dimmed the coffee chain's appeal and cut into profits. He called MyStarbucksIdea .com part of his "transformation agenda."

The site—which was inspired by Dell's IdeaStorm and works in much the same way—generated more than seventy thousand ideas in its first year. In the fall of 2010, Starbucks announced that it had implemented one hundred of the MyStarbucksIdea suggestions, including the introduction of small "splash sticks" that plug the hole in the top of their plastic cup lids, a free birthday coffee for people who have Starbucks cards, and the availability of gluten-free pastries. By partnering with its customers and being responsive to its users, the company began a turnaround.

COMMUNITY MAINTENANCE

IdeaStorm and MyStarbucksIdea are examples of customer communities spearheaded by corporations—something that's increasingly common now that virtually every company has a Facebook page. But effective customer communities require a serious investment—if user suggestions languish with no company feedback or response, the sites can backfire. User suggestions left unanswered quickly sour the brand's reputation.

As a result, commitment to the user must be genuine and long lasting. Starbucks, for example, has dedicated the time and money necessary to keep its community vibrant. The company employs more than forty "idea partners" to monitor MyStarbucksIdea.com. Each one receives special training and acts as a host on the site, responding to customer questions and guiding discussions. Chris Bruzzo, the company's chief technology officer, compares the "idea partners" to dinner party hosts responsible for making sure that everyone enjoys themselves. "Don't underinvest," Bruzzo warns. "See it as an important part of how you run your business." In a similar vein, Starbuck's Twitter feed is managed by a real person, Brad Nelson, a former barista, who goes to great efforts to make sure the Twitter feed feels authentic and part of a real coffee community.

THE FEEDBACK LOOP

Digital "suggestion boxes" such as MyStarbucksIdea are great ways to engage users in the process of improving your customer service and even your products, but what about solving the problems of those customers who don't volunteer information? For every user who takes the time to post a suggestion, you can bet there are dozens, if not hundreds more who have something to say, but aren't taking the time to express it in writing.

Some companies make use of the Net Promoter Score, a metric developed by Satmetrix, Bain & Company, and Fred Reichheld. It was introduced by Reichheld in his 2003 *Harvard Business Review* article "The One Number You Need to Grow." The concept has been embraced by companies worldwide and has become a standard for measuring and improving customer loyalty. Procter & Gamble, General Electric, eBay, Intuit, and Verizon Wireless have all used the Net Promoter Score.

The score is culled from a survey in which customers are asked one question: "How likely is it that you would recommend our company to a friend or colleague?" Based on their responses, customers are categorized into three groups: Promoters (9–10 rating), Passives (7–8 rating), and Detractors (0–6 rating). The percentage of Detractors is then subtracted from the percentage of Promoters to obtain a Net Promoter score. A score of 50 to 80 percent is considered high. Companies can follow the initial question with a request for elaboration on the reasons why the customer would or wouldn't recommend them. The findings can then be provided to front-line employees and management teams for follow-up action. Ideally with this practice, the number of Promoters will increase and the number of Detractors will decrease. Net Promoter underscores the truism of customer satisfaction: truly happy customers will refer a product to their friends.

But companies can get insights into user experiences and preferences without even asking for them. Every user visiting your Web site leaves a digital trail, providing all the information you need to identify his or her goal, whether it's being met, and if not, why. As we've discussed in previous chapters, these valuable bread crumbs are known as analytics. And Digital Leadership Set companies such as Google and JetBlue use them as a low-cost way of conducting market research. The best companies regularly analyze this data to learn how people use their digital footprint, then in response they make iterative improvements in usability, watch for resulting changes in the user data, and then start over again. This is called the "feedback loop." And they use it to continually increase the usability of their digital footprint to ultimately improve their overall performance. But every insight from the feedback loop isn't necessarily a small one. Some of these data-based insights can save a business from millions of dollars in customer-service missteps.

In 2008, Cellular South, the largest privately owned wireless communications provider in the United States with roughly eight-hundred seventy-four thousand customers in Mississippi and parts of Tennessee, Alabama, and Florida was concerned that it was not effectively promoting its online business. Offline, the company was generally known for providing excellent customer service—people who care, a local touch, southern hospitality. But online, sales needed to improve.

Cellular South originally thought the problem was a marketing issue. But analytics showed that while users were logging on, they were not completing the purchase process once they got to a page where they were supposed to select a plan. This meant Cellular South didn't have a marketing problem; it had a customer-service challenge.

To delve into the issue further, the Cellular South team conducted a usability test. They brought a series of individuals into a usability lab with a moderator who asked each person a series of questions and assigned them a variety of tasks to perform on Cellular South's Web site, including the purchase of a phone. The team watched as users were challenged to complete a purchase online. The plans were not always easy to understand and the site navigation was not intuitive.

The redesign process focused on streamlining the path users would take to make a purchase and making the site more usable. The proof of its success came at the end of the redesign. When the site launched, Cellular South customers were able to exhibit their natural shopping behaviors—one that ended up being equal parts full-service and self-service. More people began ordering phones online and then picking them up in-store, demonstrating that they took a do-it-yourself approach to their purchases—something that was discovered through astute analysis of user behavior through analytics.

By addressing its online sales challenge not as a marketing problem but as a usability issue, Cellular South brilliantly dodged a bullet that for many companies would have been a direct hit. Many companies, once something is deemed a marketing issue, continue to spend on marketing, often increasing and increasing the budget trying to solve the problem. But no matter how much a company spends on marketing, if its customers aren't able to buy or aren't comfortable buying its products, sales will not be amply buoyed. This is a mistake many businesses make. But usability is really just another word for "online customer service." Improving your site's usability translates into providing customers with better service and makes any marketing effort much more effective.

The connection between customer service, marketing, and usability is so fundamental it's nearly impossible to talk about one without the other. A highly usable site naturally provides customers with the services they need—whether it's a clearly visible and inviting phone number for full-service users or an ample collection of accessible self-service content and tools for the DIY user. These satisfied customers are then happy users, many of whom write influential reviews online, provide highly visible recommendations to their Facebook friends, and ultimately shape the expansive and ever-present conversation about your brand marketing.

The ecosystem of external user touch points is tightly interrelated. Without a user-centric sales environment, utility marketing, and a brand-differentiating higher calling product, many users won't even get to the customer-service stage. To gain maximum returns from the internal user-centric drivers such as user-centric management, concentric organization, and disposable technology, these external touch points must all be employed and should function in relative harmony so they are all pushing the same user-first message. When this happens, the company is authentically, transparently, and wholly dedicated to its users—and for this dedication users will open their wallets, continue the chain of good word of mouth, and elevate overall company performance.

CHAPTER SUMMARY:
BILATERAL CUSTOMER SERVICE

Market Insight

- Today's customers have a strong self-service mentality—they want to be able to do everything themselves and solve every problem without human intervention. This mentality is getting stronger among younger generations who are more at home with digital technology.

- Today's customers also have a strong full-service mentality—when self-service fails, they demand immediate, personal support with a real person.

- Thanks to social media, a customer-service issue is also a marketing issue, as one complaint posted on Facebook can live online forever. Companies can no longer get away with bad customer service and expect people not to know about it.

Strategic Imperative

- User-first companies understand that to address user needs they must implement "bilateral customer service." This means offering extremely high levels of self-service, where any information a user needs can easily be found online, and any task is easily to accomplish digitally—and providing equally accessible, friendly, and helpful human service, which can be in stores, on the phone, or by chat.

- A human and transparent approach is always most effective when addressing customer-service issues. Consumers will forgive companies for any transgression provided the response is sincere, genuine, and helpful.

- Good customer service online is no different than that provided offline. It's about thinking about user needs and meeting them by volunteering need-to-know information as well as a caring approach to problem solving. User-first companies make it clear that there are real people behind the company's brand who are trying to do the right thing.

CONCLUSION

Making the Shift

It's Not Too Late to Become a User-First Organization

As I speak to companies about becoming a user-first business, I am often asked about the two biggest issues that influence everything in life: time and money. Regarding time, the question is, "Is it too late for my company? Am I just too far behind? When should I do a certain digital initiative?" And on the subject of money, it's always about how much or how little to spend. The short answer to both is that it's not too late and you have enough money to make your business user-first. The long answer is a bit more nuanced and complex.

TIMING

Take solace in these two facts: first, you are not alone in your concerns. Since so few companies are true market leaders in the digital space, the rest of the business world feels as if it's playing catch-up. Second, doing something first online doesn't give you an advantage. That's a myth left over from the dot-com boom.

In the late 1990s, the business world was bewitched with the simplistic idea that if a company got onto the Internet in front of its competitors, it would be able to grab the market, own the category in the minds of consumers, and gain an unassailable lead. This mindset inspired venture capitalists to funnel money into half-baked ideas and start-ups to hastily file for IPOs. But these quick moves to action didn't create many overnight billionaires. In fact most fast players burned their own money and that of their investors. Being first just wasn't that much of a competitive advantage. If it were, we'd all be using our Netscape browsers to get to the Web sites of Webvan and Kozmo. But we're not. The latter two companies went bankrupt in 2001 and powerhouses such as Diapers.com and FreshDirect grew in their wake. And Google Chrome is a far cry from Netscape.

Take a look at the following list of industry leaders and identify which were the first of their kind to market:

- Google

- YouTube

- Facebook

- Apple's iPod

- Skype

The answer: none.
Each of these leading companies left behind a raft of early movers.

- Google came after Infoseek, WebCrawler, Yahoo, and Lycos

- YouTube followed Xing Technology and RealVideo

- Facebook launched after Friendster and MySpace

- Apple's iPod was beat to the market by the Diamond Rio and Creative Labs Nomad

- Skype came after Vocaltec

Looking back at the market with twenty-twenty hindsight, it's clear that winning isn't about being first. The race for market dominance is much more intricate and subtle than that. It's about timing.

THE DIFFERENCE BETWEEN A BILLION-DOLLAR COMPANY AND BANKRUPTCY

Groupon was launched in October 2008 by Andrew Mason, a University of Chicago dropout. Less than two years later, *Forbes* published a cover story about the start-up called "Meet the Fastest Growing Company Ever"—on track to reach annual revenues of $1 billion faster than any business in history.

As you are probably aware, Groupon is a group-buying site, the name appropriately a mash-up of "group" and "coupon." It offers daily bargains on products and services sold by local merchants, now in more than forty-three countries. Often the deal is 50 to 90 percent off regular prices. But there's a catch. The deals aren't valid until a minimum number of people buy in—not sign up but actually agree to pay up front for it. It might be something like: spend $75 now for a coupon that's good for $150 at a gourmet restaurant or a spa. If enough people put the $75 down, the deal is on. If not, it simply expires, and no credit cards are charged. To publicize the promotions, Groupon posts them on their site, sends them out through social media, and delivers them to subscribers via e-mail. If users see a deal they want that's not "on" yet, they'll be inclined to share it with their friends. In this way, Groupon harnesses the power of individual users' social networks to deliver their advertising message and that of their local partners. The local merchants participate because they're guaranteed a minimum number of customers from the deal. They know what their margins will be, how their brand awareness will be boosted, and they decide it's worth it. Then Groupon makes money by grabbing a cut from the deals it sells.

The company's first daily promotion was a two-for-one deal at a pizza joint located in the same Chicago building as its office. Twenty people took the offer. Two months later, Groupon had attracted four hundred subscribers. And two years later, in December 2010, the number had swelled to more than forty-four million. That month, three million new subscribers signed up in just one week, and Google offered Mason $6 billion for the company. He turned it down, raising $950 million from private equity firms a few months later. Soon thereafter, it became one of the year's most anticipated IPOs.

As you might expect from the theme of this chapter, Groupon wasn't a first. The group-buying concept had been tried unsuccessfully a decade before by a Bellevue, Washington, company called Mercata.

Mercata launched in May 1999, with the slogan, "If you're not part of the we-commerce revolution, you're history!" The start-up, led by an experienced management team, partnered with more than three hundred companies to offer deals on everything from computers to luggage. It was based on almost the same idea as Groupon—that pooling consumers together would result in bulk discounts and be good for both the consumers and the retailers. Unlike Groupon, however, the more people who signed up for a particular product, the cheaper it would go.

As it turned out, the "we-commerce" revolution was short and bloody. Mercata shut down at the end of January 2001 after burning eighty-nine million dollars in venture capital in twenty months.

What we have here is essentially the same idea a decade apart with the pioneer fading into obscurity and the follower storming into the market and becoming the toast of the business press. How'd this happen? Mercata had bad timing. The technology required to create a group-buying service that would be valuable to a large market didn't exist when it broke ground in 1999.

Here's how a decade makes a huge difference:

- In the late 1990s, relatively few local businesses were concerned with developing a Web presence. It just wasn't on their radar. Mercata therefore had its original sights set on striking deals with national companies for products like TVs and cameras, and then it had to compete head-to-head on pricing with retailers such as Walmart and Target because they sold the same things. But Mercata deals weren't always good enough to wait for. And, without social networking or instant access to e-mail via smart phones, Mercata's deals spread so slowly, they could take days to tip. This left time for consumers to find adequate deals elsewhere without the wait. There was little compelling reason for people to use the service.

- By 2008, almost every mom-and-pop store had some kind of Web presence or felt the need to market using the Internet. This enabled Groupon to enter local markets and avoid direct competition with retail giants. Then, because of the prevalence of social networking in users' everyday lives, consumers were receptive to the group-buying concept and were able to spread deals quickly. Groupon's promotions would tip within a few hours. And then Groupon could start all over again the next day with a new set of deals—a frequency that functioned to drive engagement with its users.

Groupon shows that first-to-market does not win; it's the company that is first to launch a great user experience *when* the technology makes it possible and customers are ready to buy:

- **Technology:** Above anything else, for a new digital product to have a chance at greatness, the technology environment must be ready for it. This means the technology must be able to support an exceptional user experience, mass-mass market adoption, and affordable scalability. For Groupon, the pervasiveness of e-mail, Twitter and Facebook, and the Web savvy of local businesses drove its ability to provide great deals to consumers and activate a ready and willing mass market.

- **User experience over customer experience:** Users need a compelling reason to try out a new product, let alone to become a customer. Without a good, valuable user-centric experience, there's no way to become a category leader. Groupon created the best possible experience for group buying. It always presented users with exciting, almost too-good-to-be-true bargains, and produced these deals at a frequency that gave the impression it always had something else great just around the corner.

- **Mass-market adoptability:** If the technology exists to power your product, but most people don't have it yet, you don't have a market. If you have a great, innovative, groundbreaking idea, but it doesn't match a mass-market frame of reference, you also don't have a market. What's more, at the end of the day, you don't need just a market, you need a paying one. Some patient investors might allow a site to gain traction before monetizing it, but eventually bills will have to be paid. For Groupon, local business owners were Web savvy enough to recognize and welcome the innovative way to attract new customers. Users, accustomed to buying online and to time-sensitive online deals, were primed to put their money down.

Companies need to watch for the "perfect storm" as it relates to their business. When the timing is right, the revenue model will click at the same time as the technology environment. This is what has enabled some of the most significant advancements in the last twenty years.

TECHNOLOGY DEVELOPMENT, ADOPTION, AND MARKET OPPORTUNITIES

Over time, we've all observed that computers get faster, hard drives get bigger, and our Internet access gets quicker. Looking at these trends in reverse, we can see that the price of processing power, storage, and bandwidth has been declining over time: as computers get faster, the price of processing power declines by about a third each year; as mobile and broadband connectivity becomes more ubiquitous, the price of bandwidth drops about 5 percent a year; and storage costs fall about 37 percent a year. So we have an exponential decline in price over time.

This downward curve—what I call the digital enablement curve—can explain the emergence of virtually all big innovations in the digital space. Each time one of these factors has become inexpensive enough to allow a particular technology to emerge, we've taken a huge step forward. For example, the World Wide Web only began to enter the home in 1994 after personal computer power had increased to the point where at-home computers could handle Internet protocols, making connection to the Web easy; Napster, and file sharing in general, took off in 1999 as use of high-bandwidth channels started to become widely available and affordable; YouTube emerged in 2005 just as storage became cheap enough to allow for free video hosting.

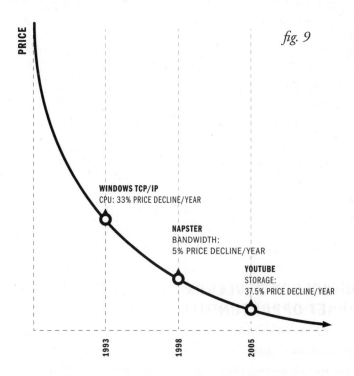

fig. 9

PRICE

WINDOWS TCP/IP
CPU: 33% PRICE DECLINE/YEAR

NAPSTER
BANDWIDTH:
5% PRICE DECLINE/YEAR

YOUTUBE
STORAGE:
37.5% PRICE DECLINE/YEAR

1993 1998 2005

9. The Digital Enablement Curve

So when thinking about launching a new product or entering a new market, consider the digital enablement curve. It explains why so many similar products launch at the same time. When you, the entrepreneur or innovator in your company, think of something new and amazing to launch, you're not the only genius in the world who's come to the same conclusion. Because it's likely only been a recent phenomenon that technology made this new idea possible. The result is that many grab this new market opportunity. But only a few come out on top. And when all those players jump into this new market and jockey for position, user experience tends to be the driver that enables one company to dominate.

USER EXPERIENCE: THE POINT OF DIFFERENCE

Groupon isn't the only daily deals site out there, nor was it the first, but it may be the only one you've ever bought anything from. Since the environment allowed for daily deals, these types of sites have multiplied at a rate that's almost impossible to track. In mid-2011, Yipit, which tracks daily deals in the same way Kayak aggregates fares from travel sites, was following bargains on 535 daily bargain sites, up from 291 bargain sites just three months earlier. Their pool included Groupon as well as competitors such as LivingSocial, BuyWithMe, Woot, and Tippr. Groupon has been hanging on as the leader. No one else who leapt to market when the getting was good was able to produce a user experience so compelling.

This tends to be the rule: the digital property that offers a great user experience *first* often gains mass adoption and loyal customers. If the leader is then able to engage and lock in users fast enough to develop a network effect, this win could last into the long term—even if its user experience lags a bit in innovation over time, the network effect will keep it strong. A competitor will not be able to steal audience from the market winner unless a new experience comes along that is dramatically better than the competition—so much better that new users flock to it and existing users and customers are motivated to switch. If it's incrementally better, no one will bother to make the change because the effort involved to switch just isn't worth it. For example, one can argue that today there are many places that provide a better shopping experience than Amazon—Amazon, for example, does a poor job with product photography and providing very detailed product specifications. But Amazon is simple and the experience is good enough, so it's remained in a strong leadership position. But complacency by the leader could result in a situation where the user experience degrades so much that a newcomer with a great user experience can come in, appear revolutionary, and motivate users to switch. Harking back to Quicken and Mint in chapter 1, once upon a time Quicken was perceived as an amazingly usable product—much better than paper. Then it became so increasingly unusable that Mint's elegant usability was revolutionary enough to force change. Today, some think this is happening at Google: it is a good search experience, but one that's littered with low-quality links and is increasingly difficult to use. If the slide in quality continues, a new user experience may emerge that fosters displacement. See early semantic Web services such as Wolfram Alphra for a hint at what the revolutionary shift could be—once the digital enablement curve makes it possible.

NOT TOO EARLY, NOT TOO LATE

We see that entering a market too early can be a disaster as companies must wait for the digital enablement curve and market in general to catch up, and being too late creates a similar problem because a market leader becomes so entrenched that users have little reason to switch to an incrementally better product.

Pandora is a great example of the timing challenge—and of the value of a user-first, customer-second strategy. Tim Westergren, founder and chief strategy officer of Pandora, started out as a musician and worked for a time as a composer for films. One day in 1999, while analyzing the construction of music to predict what film directors might like, he came up with the idea of creating a music genome, basically an analysis of the construction of music that would allow for the identification of structural similarities between songs. It would be a revolutionary technology, able to recommend songs to users not solely based on genre or artist but on the actual structure and style of the music. It would have the power to introduce music fans to new artists they might never have discovered otherwise. His idea was unarguably user-first, but it would only come to fruition if he could come up with a business model and get himself supported by some paying customers. This is where he hit a wall.

His first-phase business model was to license his technology as a music recommendation service to businesses that sold music to consumers. AOL, Tower Records, Barnes & Noble, and other sites used Pandora's technology to offer music shoppers suggestions of artists or songs that were similar to their apparent preferences, something that's not dissimilar to Netflix's recommendation service. Eventually Pandora even ended up in kiosks at Best Buy retail locations.

This, however, didn't spell success. He had an idea strong in usability and had tailored it to the technology of the day, but he didn't have a large enough customer base. "It's very hard to make a profitable business when you're beholden to a small number of very large customers," he said in a 2006 interview with the site The Underground Mine. By the end of 2001, as the market crashed, Westergren's start-up went broke. He found an eviction notice taped to his office door. Workers, whom he had begged to work unpaid, began suing.

But he wasn't going to give up. He maxed out eleven credit cards, and he actually considered a company trip to Reno to gamble for more money. Meanwhile, he frantically, passionately, made hundreds of pitches to potential new investors, many of whom were burned by the market crash and unwilling to support another dot-com. Then it happened: he got a break. In March 2004, after years of dogged persistence, his 348th pitch earned him a nine-million-dollar round of funding.

As he told The Underground Mine:

> "What that allowed us to do was stop and take a breath for a second and consider, where should we really be taking this thing? What happed in those intervening years were pretty significant things. Broadband had become a much more ubiquitous phenomenon. Music on the Internet requires a nice healthy amount of pipe and doesn't work so well on dial-up. Once that had flipped over and broadband had become much more ubiquitous, online audio suddenly looked much more like a mass-market product than it had before."

Technology was now in Westergren's corner. In 2005, Pandora launched a revolutionary product. It was a consumer-facing, Web-based music player with revenues driven by advertisements and later subscriptions too. Users would make their own "radio stations" by telling Pandora the name of an artist or artists they felt like listening to, and then Pandora would immediately produce a radio station based on the artist(s) that would include other music the user would be likely to enjoy. Music enthusiasts gushed over the service. It effectively introduced music to users that they might not have discovered otherwise and that they ended up liking. It also did users a service by eliminating the difficult task of deciding what music to download and listen to—a hard choice to make when there is an unlimited amount of music available online. In this way, it functioned similarly to Google; it smartly curated an infinite volume of material for users. Westergren finally had all three factors for success in line: technology, a mass market of users, and a vast universe of advertisers (customers). And what's more, his product genuinely offered tremendous value.

But Westergren didn't get complacent basking in his long-awaited success. To stay relevant, he continued to bolster the service's user experience. In 2008, Pandora released an iPhone app that let people stream music through their phones—this meant they could listen to Pandora at the gym, on the sidewalk, anytime. Almost immediately, thirty-five thousand new users a day began joining Pandora from their mobiles, *The New York Times* reported. As of July 2010, Pandora was the most popular Internet radio service, with sixty million registered users and a 52 percent market share. It represented 1.7 percent of all radio listening—not just Web radio listening. Then Westergren made moves to get Pandora into cars. In 2011 Ford began shipping cars with software that allowed drivers to use Pandora via voice control. Mercedes-Benz was said to be offering Pandora controls on some of its steering wheels too. And Pioneer Electronics has begun to sell Pandora-ready car stereos.

In February 2011, Pandora filed to go public. Its financials showed that for the first nine months of 2010, Westergren's company attracted ninety million dollars in revenue, an increase of thirty million dollars over the same months in 2009. Pandora does have competitors—such as Last.fm, Grooveshark, and Slacker Radio—that sprang up when the technology and mass market came into being. But Pandora's constant innovation in reaction to the technology marketplace has made it far and away the winner.

This story has a happy ending, primarily due to Westergren's perseverance, commitment to constant improvement, and innately user-first innovation. But Pandora did nearly die a horrible death because it entered the scene too early, a full decade before technology and a market were really there to support it.

Companies have just as much of a challenge when they enter a market late, after the first great user experience has entered a market and dominated. That's the challenge faced by Microsoft's search engine Bing.

Microsoft launched Bing in 2009 to compete directly with Google. Bing had a monumental challenge primarily because consumers were happy with Google; so happy that its name has become a verb in the public lexicon. While weaknesses were emerging in Google's search experience, it was nothing serious enough to motivate a user to switch to a different provider.

In launching Bing, Microsoft did what any new market entrant tries to do: it made a better product. While we can debate whether Microsoft succeeded in making Bing better than Google, Bing did make incremental improvements to the search experience. It would synthesize data such as user reviews to produce information the user was looking for rather than a simple list of search results. It offered a full-service travel reservation system. It also incorporated some semantic Web technologies, which means that the search engine would better understand the context of what users were searching for to recommend different or better search terms. But incremental improvement wasn't enough. To try to get more traction in the market Microsoft spent an estimated hundred million dollars to advertise Bing, a remarkable amount considering that Google's ad budget for all of 2008 was only twenty-five million dollars. The campaign, however, was basically a giant exercise in convincing consumers that they had a problem with search, and that only Bing could solve it—a problematic proposition because consumers had no real problem with search; people were happy with Google.

Not surprisingly, attempting to convince people that Google's search wasn't good enough was not enough to topple the giant. *Wired*'s Ryan Singel wrote at Bing's launch, "It doesn't quite go far enough to make us feel that it's time to dump Google." And then to fight back, Google simply copied and incorporated many of Bing's innovations. By the end of 2010, the upstart hadn't dented Google's lead—Google still controlled more than 66 percent of the U.S. search-engine market, a higher share than when Bing was launched. Bing had attracted 12 percent of the market, but the converts didn't come from Google, they came from Yahoo! and other sites.

If there's already a strong market leader and the new product doesn't offer a substantially improved user experience, the most likely outcome is a long, expensive battle for market share in which the field is tilted against the new entrant.

WHAT TIMING MEANS FOR YOUR BUSINESS

I've made the argument that effectively entering a new market is about good timing; it's not about being the first, nor is it sly to wait so long that a Goliath has time to form in your path. But admittedly not being first can be a scary thing. How many business plans are rejected because the market gets evaluated as too cluttered? You're sitting across from a VC at a posh Japanese restaurant. You pitch him your idea, and he says, "I've heard that before. Tell me something new." You're standing at the end of a boardroom table and your board chairman says, "Why are you trying to make something that already exists?" You're on the phone with a prominent technology journalist, and she says with a yawn, "Doesn't so-and-so, and so-and-so, and so-and-so do that already? Not sure I can sell that to my editor."

But this type of environment is often the most fertile for success— over time, the companies that emerge as winners are generally those that offer better user experiences in existing markets that do not yet already have an established market leader. The existence of competition, as long as it's not entrenched, is generally a sign that a market is ripe for such a service. Embracing user-first management "late" to the party can also be seen as a good way to learn from the errors of everyone else. Think back to our discussion in chapter 7 about sales. Today there are proven models to selling online; think how many businesses failed in e-commerce before those models were perfected and could be followed by others.

Really, in spite of how the critics may initially react, it's truly not too late for your business. The twenty years of the Web is a mere blip in business history. It's up to the talented user-centric manager to sell this reality.

MONEY

I'll now shift focus to briefly discuss the other question that's on everyone's mind: the cost of investment to become a user-first business.

Here's the key thing to remember when it comes to investing in digital technology: virtually every company that exists has a digital-only firm attempting to compete against them. And these digital-only players are smart, savvy, and will spend what it takes to win. They're either technology giants who have so much money that cash problems never enter the equation, or they're backed by venture capitalists who are telling them to spend more to get big faster. Until you've been inside one of these companies or start-ups it is impossible to understand or appreciate their will to win.

A decade ago, I was running Silverpop Systems, an e-mail service provider that I started in my bedroom and that went on to raise more than thirty-five million dollars in venture funding. After we received our first round of investment, we had our first quarterly board meeting. I presented our company financials, proud of the fact that we were being responsible managers and staying under budget. The response from the venture capitalists sitting in the room was one of panic: what was going on, what was wrong with the business? Why weren't we spending fast enough? Are we having trouble hiring? Is there a marketing problem? Is there an issue with acquiring the requisite hardware? The point was: the money was there to build a successful business—and the bigger and faster we could do it, the better off we'd all be.

Facebook is another example of this approach to money and growth: its limiting factor to success is not money, but the talent and resources to get things done. So it's literally buying companies—like the recently acquired start-up drop.io—not for the product, technology, or customers, but for the talent. It's spending millions of dollars to attract talented groups of people who can build great user experiences. Facebook wins and keeps on winning because it can afford not to compromise; it can be fully dedicated to making great products and experiences that users will fall in love with.

Compare this spending ethos to your business: your company has limited budget and resources. You probably have to fight for every dollar of budget you get; hiring new people is a big deal; and in many companies, human resource policies make firing someone even harder. To compound matters, it's even more difficult to get approval for things that need ongoing, long-term financial support. When an investment is approved, it's often thought of as a one-time expense. As a result, the ongoing management and improvement of the endeavor is short-funded.

Another problem in procuring sufficient funds for digital technology investments is that budgets typically go to what's already proven—spending more on the organization's core business and core economic engine, instead of something that's perceived as new and with unproven returns. For this reason, most companies don't allocate enough money to digital technology to really set the stage for successful user-centric management. They don't see the Internet as part of their core business and they're more comfortable making major investments in already mature, proven areas that eke out small, reliable returns. So even when someone comes to them with clear and concise math illustrating the magnitude of the opportunity in digital media and the risk to their core business if they don't make the shift, they still feel uneasy. They see a large expenditure with an incredibly big theoretical return—and this makes them feel as if they're missing something in the fine print, that risks are being omitted from the sales pitch. So they dial down the spend and go conservative, underfunding the initiative often to the point that it can't reach its full potential and teeters on failure. This is why a brick-and-mortar retailer rolls out new stores, while it leaves its digital footprint vulnerable. It's why an airline invests in expanding its route map, while allowing its Web site to remain confusing and frustrating for potential new passengers. And as long as this safe and outdated dynamic continues in your organization, you're doomed.

To make things more difficult for companies, even when executives do decide to go big on digital, because organizations are often so set in their ways, this strategic decision does not translate into how money is actually spent. Recently I was at an executive-level meeting discussing the future of a brand. At the meeting, it was agreed that the organization would put increased focus on digital media—specifically, a big push into e-commerce with the goal of building a direct, higher-margin relationship with its end customer. It was agreed that this was critical to the brand's survival and the competitiveness of the overall organization. Everyone left happy. Strategic problem solved.

But my next meeting with that company—a week later—was with managers two levels down the ladder to discuss actual budgets and resources to get the job done. In this meeting, I heard a dramatically different story. It turned out the brand had a bad year and so they needed to cut budgets—and this meant there was no money to fund the new initiative that would turn the company into an e-commerce powerhouse. Senior management wanted the shift to e-commerce, but that request never translated into a change in budgets. Three months later, the brand's marketing manager is still in a holding pattern, scrounging for funds. Mind you, this company is by no means poor. It is one of the largest companies in the world. And this situation isn't unique. It's something I see all the time. It's not uncommon for top-level executive leadership to be disconnected from how the money is actually being allocated and spent.

MONEY IS NOT ESSENTIAL

For the majority of businesses small and large, money for a new digital technology initiative is a limited commodity. But this doesn't mean a user-first strategy is out of reach. Millions of dollars is helpful, don't get me wrong, but it's not necessary. Valuable elements of a user-first strategy are within reach for small businesses, nonprofits, and departments functioning on a tight budget. Think back to chapter 2, "Concentric Organization." Creating a strong digital core, which empowers employees, guarantees a high-quality user experience for audiences, and ultimately affects user-first change across the organization, requires only a small team of engineers and designers. Many of the success stories referenced in chapter 3, "Disposable Technology," relied on free software and again, small, focused teams. Utility marketing is also readily available for businesses on a budget. My mother, a dentist, runs a small business. So she spends her time, or at least asks me to spend my time, thinking about how to make her dental office user-first. While some things cannot be justified from an investment standpoint (for example, there's no good way to allow her patients to sign up for dental appointments online), she has been able to make a big impact when it comes to marketing. By applying utility marketing (particularly through the use of search and social) to her dental practice and thinking about her Web site (DrTerryShapiro.com) as a destination in the unified traffic framework, she has been able to transform her business. Today, the majority of her new patients come from the Internet, and patient follow-ups are initiated digitally.

Aspects of TCPF (trust, convenience, price, fun) sales, and bilateral customer service are also achievable for those on a tight budget. Anyone as big as Target or as small as Geroy's can sell his or her goods through Amazon. And anyone can spend a few hours putting herself in the shoes of someone completely unfamiliar with her business to add informative FAQs to her Web site.

For some resources to get you started, take a look at my Web site, AaronShapiro.com, which has many articles, blog posts, resources, and links about user-first management. My company's Web site also has thought leadership (www.hugeinc.com) that can help inform a digital strategy. I also suggest taking a look at some of the great usability resources that exist online, such as usability.gov and useit.com. Finally, there's no better way to see how your company should evolve than by getting a pulse of the technology start-up scene—go to local meet-ups and check out tech blogs and link aggregators such as TechMeme.com. And to truly see the future of what users want, talk to your local college students or better yet, their younger teenage siblings. Watch how they use digital. Before long, that'll be mainstream.

LOVE

On an office wall at HUGE, we have a big poster that says "Make Something You Love." The idea is simple: we're a company full of people who make great digital experiences; if you make something great that you really care about and really love, the users will follow. Think about the experiences online that you love: you like them because of all the little things that make them simple, intuitive, and great. It's as if the application were reading your mind, anticipating your every move, making sure that you're happy. That feeling didn't happen by accident; it happened because someone at the company who made that experience—someone in the digital core—labored away, sweating all the details, to make sure that you'd be happy with the experience. She put her heart and soul into it and something beautiful was created.

That's the secret to the success of a user-first business—not money, not genius, not unending perseverance. Just love. You must perceive your users as you perceive yourself, as a full-fledged, breathing, thinking, smart, critical human being simply looking for ways to live a happier, more stress-free, and enjoyable life. Your users, just like you, will choose happiness over anything else every time. And on the Internet, users have power to choose and they do so with every click. To win, you simply must create a digital experience that you'd love to use—because it saves you time, is intuitive in its design, provides fun or laughter, saves you money, gives you social interaction, or anything else—and all your users will love it too. It's about building an experience that meets people's true inner needs; marketing that's in the service of users, instead of trying to trick them; a sales channel that's simple and gives people the confidence they're buying the right thing; and a customer-service experience that's genuinely trying to help. And behind all this, a management, organizational structure, and technical infrastructure that keeps the love and care alive. Share the love, and your business will thrive.

ACKNOWLEDGMENTS

This book would not have been possible without a tremendous team behind me. I would like to thank Willow Duttge, who did an incredible job helping me research, write, and edit the book; Doug Merlino for his invaluable research and editorial support; Bhaskar Chitraju and Justin Sunga for driving the Digital Leadership Set research survey; Joe Stewart for the cover design and Jorge Balarezo for book illustrations; Sam Weston for his strategie counsel; my literary agent, Rebecca Friedman; and the entire Portfolio Penguin team, particularly Adrian Zackheim and Courtney Young. Thanks to everyone at HUGE—the amazing things you do every day are a big inspiration for this book. I'd also like to thank the current and past clients of HUGE, some of whom are discussed in this book, including American Society of Mechanical Engineers, Cellular South, Comcast, IKEA, JetBlue Airways, National Association of Realtors, Nutrisystem, NYC & Company, Penton Media, PepsiCo, Pizza Hut, and Thomson Reuters. Finally, much appreciation to my family—Carolyn, Sam, and Benjamin—who were so supportive throughout the entire process.

APPENDIX:
The Digital Leadership Set Survey

In preparation for this book, I tasked my research team with a grand challenge: rank all of the Fortune 1,000 on the degree to which they are effective in digital, and use this data to find patterns that underscore digital excellence. To add to the challenge, it was important that the survey was completely quantitative in nature; we did not want subjective factors to enter into our determination of digital leadership. The survey was a two-step process.

Our first step in establishing the Digital Leadership Set was to select a pool of companies to evaluate. For this we used the Fortune 1,000 for 2010. These top-performing businesses undoubtedly interact with large numbers of users and have the financial wherewithal to create powerful user-first experiences. But most important, these companies were all already exhibiting effective management as proven by the universal measure of success: revenue generation.

Next we needed to consolidate the Fortune 1,000 into comparable industries. As is, the Fortune 1,000 includes a motley crew of seventy-five industries—everything from tobacco to medical facilities, Internet services and mining. If we were to compare the user-first, digital progressiveness of these industries on the same level playing field, it surely wouldn't be a fair fight. Presumably companies that were more industrial in nature and less consumer-facing wouldn't have seen as much need to invest in a user-first digital strategy. So to be sure we were comparing apples to apples, and to make sure we had enough companies within each industry to make single-industry indexes meaningful, we broke the Fortune 1,000 into nineteen industries (shown below). Then within these industries we evaluated the top twenty companies, based on revenue, to make sure we were evaluating companies of comparable scale. (Some industries still consisted of significantly fewer than twenty firms. As a result, we evaluated 349 companies in total.)

Industry	Includes But Is Not Limited To . . .
Aerospace and Defense	Commercial and military grade airplanes, satellites, intelligence, and surveillance
Automotive	Motor vehicle manufacturers, sales, rental, and parts
Beauty and Apparel	Clothing and makeup brands
Business Services	Temporary help, outsourcing services, and facilities management
Consumer Products and Services	Household product and appliance manufacturers, services for the home
Diversified Holding Companies	Firms that hold interests in a wide variety of industries
Energy	Producers of oil and electricity
Financial Services	Investment banks and insurance

Industry	Includes But Is Not Limited To . . .
Food and Beverage	Food and beverage producers, tobacco
Health Care	Pharmaceutical producers and distributors
Industrials	Construction and farm machinery providers as well as chemical and metal producers
Media and Entertainment	Producers of print, television, music, movie, and radio content as well as advertising companies
Real Estate	Commercial and residential real estate services
Retail	Physical retail stores including drugstores, big-box stores, and department stores
Technology	Computer and electronics equipment, Internet services and retailing, and software
Telecommunications	Network, phone, Internet, television, and communications equipment providers
Transportation and Logistics	Trucking, truck leasing, railroads, and delivery services
Travel and Leisure	Airlines, hotels, casinos, and resorts
Utilities	Providers of gas, electric, and other utilities to residential and commercial properties

With our pool of successful companies selected and the industries defined, we needed to create a system through which we could evaluate and quantify a company's digital expertise. This required identifying which user-first qualities could be measured across companies and industries with as little room for subjective reasoning as possible. As a result, we focused on quantitative variables across all "public facing" areas of digital: company Web site, corporate communications, customer service, mobile, products, sales, search, and social. In total, we defined sixty-one quantitatively measurable variables across the eight categories:

- **Company Web Site** evaluated the fundamental quality of a corporation's own Web site. Did the site include clear navigation, search functionality, information for the press and investors? And more advanced: did it have multilingual support or the ability for users to create accounts and maintain profiles?

- **Social** included an in-depth analysis of each company's participation and influence in social media extending through Facebook, Twitter, YouTube, and LinkedIn. Did the company have a Twitter account? How frequently did it tweet? How many "likes" did it have on Facebook? How many subscribers did its YouTube channel have versus the number of visitors its channel page got? Did it effectively promote any other digital properties through these platforms?

- **Corporate Communications** included an assessment of the company's production of digital content. For example, did it have a blog or a newsletter? Was it well maintained? How was the content distributed?

- **Customer Service** appraised the level of support available to existing or prospective customers online. How clear and easy was it to find the company's contact information? Did it have a live chat option?

- **Mobile** judged the activity level of the company in mobile technology including apps and sites optimized for the mobile viewing environment.

- **Products** evaluated whether the company used digital technology to enhance offline products.

- **Sales** measured the comprehensiveness of product information available online and if the site was structured so customers could easily purchase products and services.

- **Search** reviewed the prominence of the company in search results via both paid and organic search.

Company Web site and social categories each accounted for 20 percent of the company's final score. The remaining six categories each accounted for 10 percent of a company's ratings.

One by one we evaluated the companies against these criteria and tallied up their scores, earning a final ranking of between one and one hundred. This would be its digital excellence ranking—the higher the ranking, the more comprehensive, robust, and user-first its digital presence. With this figure, we were then able to look at trends across the entire marketplace, pick out the leaders in digital across the top tier of the Fortune 1,000 and within specific industries, and even measure the overall digital savvy of industries themselves.

It should be noted that there is one key component of the survey that is both a strength and a weakness: the fact that every criterion we evaluated was a completely quantitative evaluation (for example, a normalized number of Twitter followers, or the existence of accessibility compliance on the Web site). We did not assess companies from a qualitative perspective—namely, how good a job they did in implementing certain initiatives. As a result, some companies scored relatively high in the Digital Leadership index when a heuristic evaluation of the execution of certain activities would suggest significant room for improvement (for example, Home Depot). Likewise, other companies scored lower than expected because the lack of certain qualitative characteristics of their activities hurt performance, even though they may have executed some activities particularly well (for example, Apple). However, we believe that these issues cause only minimal levels of deviation in the context of the overall ranking.

RESULTS

The elite Digital Leadership Set was made up of consumer-facing companies well known for being innovative and functioning primarily within the technology and retail industries:

Amazon	Hewlett-Packard	Southwest Airlines
American Express	The Home Depot	Staples
Apple	IBM	Target
Best Buy	JetBlue Airways	Walmart
Dell	Macy's	Washington Post Company
FedEx	Microsoft	Wells Fargo
Google	Sears Holdings	

To delve deeper into the trends, we evaluated the average performance of companies within each industry:

Industry	Index Per Industry (0-100)
Retail	68
Technology	58
Financial Services	54
Telecommunications	54
Travel and Leisure	49
Food and Beverage	42
Transportation and Logistics	41
Business Services	41
Beauty and Apparel	40
Media and Entertainment	38
Industrials	35
Utilities	33
Energy	32
Health Care	31

Automotive	31
Diversified Holdings	30
Aerospace and Defense	29
Real Estate	29
Consumer Products and Services	28
Overall Average	**40**

The retail industry led the pack largely because of the many ways retailers seek to connect with consumers. The retailers surveyed offered not only more online shopping functionality than any other industry but more mobile apps and produced more social media activity, primarily through Facebook. Technology companies, on the other hand, ranked near the top in part because they offered users highly usable customer service options. Live chat, blogs, and online discussion forums were more present in these companies than in any other industry. We can assume consumer products and services performed the lowest because these companies largely operate in the digital environment more as manufacturers of consumer goods than as consumer-facing companies. While popular brand names such as Procter & Gamble and Kimberly-Clark were present in the industry list, so were companies that consumers are less familiar with like Masco and Jarden. When the consumer population is taken out of the pool of users, companies often do not establish as robust digital communications.

It is therefore interesting to examine digital leadership by industry:*

Aerospace and Defense	Boeing
	Raytheon
Automotive	General Motors
	Ford

---

* Real estate and diversified holdings is excluded as they didn't include enough companies for the top two to show meaningful levels of leadership.

Beauty and Apparel	Fossil
	Guess
Business Services	Iron Mountain
	Convergys
Consumer Products and Services	Herman Miller
	Procter & Gamble
Energy	Baker Hughes
	Murphy Oil
Financial Services	American Express
	Wells Fargo
Food and Beverage	PepsiCo
	Coca-Cola
Health Care	Johnson & Johnson
	Pfizer
Industrials	Caterpillar
	John Deere
Media and Entertainment	Washington Post
	Walt Disney
Retail	Home Depot
	Target
Technology	Google
	Microsoft

Telecommunications	AT&T
	Time Warner Cable
Transportation and Logistics	FedEx
	UPS
Travel and Leisure	JetBlue Airways
	Southwest Airways
Utilities	Dominion Resources
	Entergy

Notably, the industry winners weren't always, or even often, those with the most revenue. Only in the automotive sector and the transportation and logistics industry did the companies with the most revenue top their industry's Digital Leadership Set. This phenomenon demonstrates the energy of challenger brands, the democratization of digital media, and the notion that money isn't the only ingredient for success—any company can build fabulous, user-centric digital media experiences. It just takes the right strategy.

NOTES

INTRODUCTION: USERS FIRST

2   **Already 41 percent of all offline retail purchases:** "Forrester Forecast: Online Retail Sales Will Grow to $250 Billion by 2014," *TechCrunch*, March 8, 2010.

13   **Current chairman and CEO Bob McDonald looked to improve the company's fortunes:** Ad Age Digital A-List: P&G, *Advertising Age*, February 27, 2011.

14   **Gillette:** Gillette.com accessed May 2011.

CHAPTER 1: USER-CENTRIC MANAGEMENT

18   **he was a stickler about his personal finances:** Interview with Aaron Patzer, *Big Think*, November 24, 2009.

18   **he fell behind on his bookkeeping:** "Aaron Patzer Makes a Mint with His Financial Website," *Investor's Business Daily*, February 22, 2011.

18   **Quicken is not quick:** "A 20-Something Makes a Mint," *The New York Times*, December 2, 2009.

19   **"so easy to use, people will actually use it:"** "Easy Money: Mint.com CEO Aaron Patzer is Merging Personal Finance with Web 2.0," *Fast Company*, December 1, 2007

20   **Patzer stood to make a twenty-dollar to sixty-dollar referral fee:** "Making a Mint," *Forbes*, April 10, 2008.

20   **Within six months, it had more than 200,000 users:** "Mint's Fresh Take on Personal Finance," *Bloomberg Businessweek*, April 17, 2008.

21   **After two years in business, Mint had attracted 1.7 million users:** "The hammer Falls on Quicken Online; Mint.com emerges solo," ZDNet, November 5, 2009.

22   **YouTube had a similar strategy:** "Mint is Yodlee's YouTube," *TechCrunch*, September 18, 2009.

23 **"When a woman walks into one of our stores":** "New Approach From Gap to Cut Down on Clicks," *The New York Times,* September 12, 2005.

24 **Three years later Lenk took another great stride:** "Gap Joins the Billion-Dollar Sales Club," *The New York Times,* February 23, 2009.

26 **Apple . . . has focused on selling . . . to individual consumers:** "Microsoft's and Apple's Product Lines Compared: This Is Why Apple Wins," *Fast Company,* May 26, 2010.

27 **Apple started winning:** "Apple Passes Microsoft as No. 1 in Tech," *The New York Times,* May 26, 2010; "Apple Says iPhone and iPad Are at Use in Most Fortune 100 Companies," AppleInsider, July 20, 2010.

28 **Journalist James Fallows visited the plant:** "China Makes, the World Takes," *The Atlantic,* July/August 2007.

30 **Exxon Mobil remains extremely profitable:** "Exxon Rejects Proposals Backed by Rockefellers," *The New York Times,* May 29, 2008.

32 **Peter Scherr:** Interview with Peter Scherr, August 2010.

40 **"We test everything at Google":** Google Enterprise page about end user experience. Accessed May 2011.

41 **"Our job is to take responsibility for the complete user experience":** "Steve Jobs Speaks Out," *Fortune,* March 2008.

CHAPTER 2: CONCENTRIC ORGANIZATION

48 **labor pool has not yet caught up:** "Once a Dyanmo, the Tech Sector Is Slow to Hire," *The New York Times,* September 6, 2010.

48 **A digital talent emergency:** "A Call for Integrated Digital Thinkers," MediaBizBloggers.com, May 25, 2010.

48 **four out of five businesses:** "Trends 2010: Staffing and Hiring for eBusiness," *Forrester Research,* May 19, 2010.

50 **Mark Zuckerberg, Facebook's founder, stressed that Facebook should be seen as a utility:** "The Future of Facebook," *Time,* July 17, 2007.

50 **Facebook . . . experience:** "Liveblogging: Designing the First Fifteen Minutes," Facebook Design blog, March 13, 2010.

55 **Reader's Digest:** Interview with Lara Bashkoff, August 2010.

60 **Penton Media:** Interview with Sharon Rowlands, October 2010.

63 **In a little more than a decade [Borders]:** "Borders's Fall from Grace," *Publishers Weekly,* February 21, 2011.

64 **"I can see where it made sense on a spreadsheet":** Borders Out of Balance: Expansion, E-commerce, Music CDs among Missteps," *Crain's Detroit Business,* February 6, 2011.

64 **Less than 3 percent of Borders' revenue:** "Limit Your Options, Limit Your Horizons: A Lesson from Borders' Bankruptcy," Forbes.com, February, 18, 2011.

70 **"It seemed crazy to us":** "Can Hulu Save Traditional TV?" *Fast Company,* November 1, 2009.

CHAPTER 3: DISPOSABLE TECHNOLOGY

77 **When the doors opened to the first Blockbuster:** "Video Venture: Taking Charge of Blockbuster," *Bloomberg Businessweek.*

78 **Netflix . . . Facebook fans:** Accessed June 2011.

81 **"The most important thing we've done":** "Biz Stone on Read/Write Talk," accessed via AVC.blogs.com.

81 **NPR . . . API:** "How NPR Is Embracing Open Source and Open APIs," *O'Reilly Radar*, July 16, 2009.

85 **Friendster:** "Wall Flower at a Web Party," *The New York Times*, October 15, 2006; "Friendster Lost Lead Because of a Failure to Scale," High Scalability blog. November 13, 2007.

86 **In a public apology, Tumblr:** "Downtime," Tumblr Staff blog, December 6, 2010.

87 **"[We were] looking at how we can help the White House":** "Whitehouse.gov re-launches on Drupal and Engages the Drupal Community at DC Users Meeting," Drupal.org, November 2009.

92 **"We don't have the layers of management approval":** "Life Inside Facebook: How Head of Developers Organizes 500 People," Guardian.co.uk, November 22, 2010.

CHAPTER 4: HIGHER CALLING PRODUCTS

101 **"We needed to be more efficient than anyone else out there":** "Diapers.com Rocks Online Retailing," *Forbes*, April 26, 2010.

101 **"We live and die by the ability to get our products shipped out as fast and at low cost as possible":** "Diapers.com Walking in Zappos' Shoes," *Wall Street Journal* Blogs., October 22, 2009.

104 **"We don't define ourselves as an office furniture company":** "Herman Miller's Creative Network," *Bloomberg Businessweek*, February 15, 2008.

104 **Chase What Matters:** "Chase Focuses on What Matters to Consumers," JPMorgan Chase & Co. press release, January 9, 2008.

104 **At the time, nearly seventy million people used online banking:** "2010 Consumer Billing and Payment Trends Survey," Fiserv, July 2010.

105 **IKEA:** IKEA.com accessed February 2011.

107 **29 percent of Americans under forty used their phones for banking:** "Online Banking: The Future of Finance," MyBankTracker.com, November 17, 2010.

110 **American Express . . . Open Forum:** openforum.com accessed May 2011.

114 **one-third of Ford buyers were sold by the option:** "Ford Adding Social Networking to Cars," *Bloomberg Businessweek*, January 7, 2010.

115 **once someone has entered five runs into the Nike Plus system:** "The Nike Experiment: How the Show Giant Unleashed the Power of Personal Metrics," *Wired*, June 22, 2009.

115 **The recommendation system is so important to Netflix:** "A $1 Million Research Bargain for Netflix, and Maybe a Model for Others," *The New York Times*, September 21, 2009.

117 **Nutrisystem:** Interview with Chris Terrill, November 2010.

119 **ASME:** Interview with Nakiso Maodza, November 2010.

CHAPTER 5: UTILITY MARKETING

125 **A Phoenix lawyer blasted out an ad about a green card lottery:** "An Ad (Gasp!) in Cyberspace," *The New York Times,* April 19, 1994.

126 **only 16 percent of U.S. Internet users click on a display ad:** "comScore and Starcom USA Release Updated 'Natural Born Clickers' Study Showing 50 Percent Drop in Number of U.S. Internet Users Who Click on Display Ads," comScore press release. October 1, 2009.

126 **In a study done at HUGE:** "Display Advertising: A User-Centered Approach," white paper for HUGE Inc., June 15, 2010.

126 **Usability expert Jakob Nielsen has explained this phenomenon:** "Banner Blindess: Old and New Findings," Jakob Nielsen's Alertbox, August 20, 2007.

129 **Pepsi Refresh Project:** Internal HUGE documents and interviews with HUGE personnel; discussions with PepsiCo sources.

138 **About.com:** Interview with Matthew Knell, November 2010.

140 *The Big Short:* Accessed on Amazon.com May 2011.

144 **Red Bull's:** Facebook page accessed May 2011.

145 **National Association of Realtors:** Interview with Anne Feder, November 2010.

CHAPTER 6: TCPF

155 **LegalZoom:** LegalZoom.com accessed May 2011.

157 **In March 2011, *New York Times* journalist Ron Lieber crystallized this decision-making process:** "Adding It Up: Amazon Ship vs. Costco Shop," *The New York Times,* March 4, 2011.

158 **Pizza Hut's iPhone app:** Accessed March 2011.

159 **By the fall of 2010, the app had been downloaded two million times:** "App for Pizza Hut Rolling in the Dough," CBSlocal.com, August 17, 2010.

159 **pharmacy . . . apps:** accessed May 2011.

160 **"Recently, I had the horrific displeasure of booking a flight":** http://www .dustincurtis.com/dear_american_airlines.html

161 **This service allows consumers to save time:** eMarketer report "Buy Online, Pick Up In-Store," December 2009.

164 **In 2008, it launched a program where users could design outfits using Wet Seal clothing and accessories:** "Wet Seal of Approval," NRF Stores, October 2010.

165 **Overstock.com:** App accessed April 2011.

165 **Etsy:** www.etsy.com/gifts accessed May 2011.

168 **Zipcar:** www.zipcar.com accessed May 2011.

171 **Redfin.com has taken this model a step further:** "The Last Stand of the 6-Percenters?" *The New York Times,* September 3, 2006.

172 **Goldman Sachs:** GoldmanSachs.com accessed May 2011.

CHAPTER 7: BILATERAL CUSTOMER SERVICE

178 **Crutchfield:** Crutchfield.com accessed May 2011.

180 **In 2007, Stanley Fish . . . sparked a debate over what today's customers want:** "Getting Coffee Is Hard to Do," *The New York Times,* August 4, 2007.

182 **Walt Disney World:** Disney.go.com accessed April 2011.

183 **NYCGO.com:** Accessed March 2011.

184 **Hewlett-Packard:** HP Support Forum h30424.www3.hp.com accessed April 2011.

186 **"make it as easy as possible for people to complain":** "Social Media Part of Best Buy CRM Strategy, But Traditional Tacts Remain," *Direct Marketing News,* June 9, 2010.

187 **Zappos:** "The Fast Company 50—2009," *Fast Company,* February 11, 2009.

188 **Google's public online forums with enraged comments:** "Google's Nexus One Phone Sparks Flood of Complaints," *USA TODAY,* January 13, 2010.

188 **In October 2009, a Yelp user named "Sean C." gave a two-star review to Ocean Avenue Books:** "Yelp Fights Make Leap to Real-World Violence, Says Reviewer," Gawker.com, November 3, 2009.

190 **Toyota also set up a video Q&A to be broadcast on Digg:** "How Toyota Helped Digg Itself Out of Trouble," *Adweek,* April 5, 2010.

191 **In January, five hundred Japanese Groupon users put money down:** "Groupon Learns Japan Ropes," *The Wall Street Journal,* January 18, 2011.

193 **On June 21, 2005, the popular blogger Jeff Jarvis . . . published a post on his BuzzMachine blog:** "Dell Learns to Listen," *Bloomberg Businessweek,* October 17, 2007.

194 **MyStarbucksIdea:** " 'Hey, Starbucks, How About Coffee Cubes?' " *Bloomberg Businessweek,* April 15, 2008.

196 **Cellular South:** Internal HUGE documents and interviews with HUGE personnel; discussions with Cellular South sources.

CONCLUSION: MAKING THE SHIFT

203 **Groupon is a group buying site:** "Meet the Fastest Growing Company Ever," *Forbes,* August 30, 2010.

206 **Groupon forty-three countries:** Groupon.com/About accessed July 2011.

204 **Mercata launched in May 1999:** "Paul Allen's E-Commerce Play: Bring the Buying Club to the Net," *Bloomberg Businessweek,* May 13, 1999.

208 **Yipit . . . 535 bargain sites:** Yipit.com/about accessed May 2011.

209 **His first phase business model:** "Tim Westergren, C.S.O. & Co-founder Pandora Interviewed by June Caldwell," *The Underground Mine,* May 16, 2006.

210 **But he wasn't going to give up:** "How Pandora Slipped Past the Junkyard," *The New York Times,* March 7, 2010.

212 **Bing did make incremental improvements:** "Hands On with Microsoft's New Search Engine: Bing, But No Boom," *Wired,* May 28, 2009.

INDEX